"After the Ice Storm" (circa March 1941)
Only surviving early Affield homestead picture.
Chickenhouse is the dark building just to the left of large spruce tree.

After Wendell Affield's mother died in 2010, he discovered a time capsule locked in the chickenhouse on his family's farm homestead in northern Minnesota. He spent six years studying, transcribing, and archiving hundreds of documents, thousands of letters and diary pages, dating back to 1822, and many long-lost photos. This is the first in a series of biography.

HERMAN
1940s Lonely Hearts Search

Marilyn and Russ,
So nice to visit with you
at Beltrami County Fair.
Wendell Affield
August 2021

WENDELL AFFIELD

Books by Wendell Affield

Muddy Jungle Rivers

A River Assault Boat Cox'n's

Memory Journey of His War in Vietnam and Return Home

Herman

1940s Lonely Hearts Search

Chickenhouse Chronicles

Book I

Wendell Affield

Whispering Petals Press, LLC

Bemidji, Minnesota

Contact: info@whisperingpetalspress.com

Published in the United States by Whispering Petals Press, LLC.

Library of Congress Control Number: 2016913645

Herman, Chickenhouse Chronicles: Book I, Wendell Affield.

Although the author and publisher have made every effort to ensure the accuracy of information contained in this book, we assume no responsibility for errors, inaccuracies, omissions, or inconsistency thereof. Any slights of people, places, or organizations are unintentional. Dialogue is reconstructed.

ISBN 978-1-945902-00-0 (paperback)

ISBN 978-1-945902-01-7 (e-book)

ISBN 978-1-945902-02-4 (PDF, includes Mail Order Bride Catalogues)

Printed in the United States of America on acid-free paper

BIO026000 BIOGRAPHY & AUTOBIOGRAPHY / Personal Memoirs:

BIO033000 BIOGRAPHY & AUTOBIOGRAPHY / People with Disabilities:SOC028000 SOCIAL SCIENCE / Women's Studies

ATTENTION CORPORATIONS, UNIVERSITIES, COLLEGES, and PROFESSIONAL ORGANIZATIONS: Quantity discounts are available on bulk purchases of this book for educational, gift purposes, or premiums for increasing magazine subscriptions or renewals. Special books or book excerpts can also be created to fit specific needs.

For information, contact Whispering Petals Press, LLC: PO Box 652, Bemidji, MN 56619-0652

info@whisperingpetalspress.com

10 9 8 7 6 5 4 3 2 1 First Edition

In memory of my stepfather, Herman.

The Fates played a cruel joke on him

Acknowledgements

Usually, the spouse is the last to receive recognition. My wife, Patti, for the past six years, has quietly supported me as I explored my family's history. She listened patiently to long conversations I had with my sister, Laurel, and my brother, Chris, as we excavated childhood events. Chris has been instrumental in his recollections of life in New York City, and later, the early years on the farm. Those memories are woven into forthcoming Chickenhouse Chronicles, Book II.

In exploring Herman's past, a few from his family offered their stories. His younger sister, Elfrieda LaDoux and her son, Roy and his wife, Sally, shared memories and old family pictures. Lorraine Hightshoe Knighton and Evelyn Hightshoe Walters, Herman's nieces; Faye Monson, Herman's childhood friend and neighbor—all offered valuable insights into his early years. Karel Knutson, a World War Two veteran, shared first person stories about Herman with me.

My visit with Steve Affield and the information from his book, *Greetings from Afar; Memories of the Reinhold Affield Family*, provided turn-of-the century background about the first Affields to arrive in this country. Beltrami County Historical Society was instrumental in supplying information about the early days in Nebish.

Thank you Scotty Allison, Beltrami County Veterans Service Officer, for helping me weave through the bureaucratic paper maze to obtain Herman's military records from National Personnel Records Center in St. Louis, Missouri. Herman's army history proved integral to understanding my stepfather's past.

Our writing group, Sue Bruns, Doug Lewandowski, Polly Scotland, Marilyn Heltzer, and Mary Lou Brandvik—thank you for your countess hours of critiquing. Sue's critiques transported me back sixty years to grammar and comp class. Angela Foster, a wonderful editor who I first met and worked with on my Vietnam memoir, provided big picture developmental edits that proved very insightful. Thank you, Angela.

My daughter, Trish, and the company she founded, TJ Studio, Bemidji, MN, has been instrumental in graphic design and formatting for my first book and this one. TJ Studio, now owned by Paul Bunyan Communications, continues to support the technical aspects of my work, website, etc. Thank you.

And finally, the late Susan Carol Hauser. Susan was an early believer in this book. She recognized the historical significance—the forerunner of today's dotcom dating sites. I shared the old lonely hearts club catalogues with her and her first response was that they were lost history—a glimpse into the risks women of our mothers' generation took. "Young women need to see these," she told me.

Contents

From the Author xxi

Prologue xxiii

Part I

Effeld (Affield) Roots 1

1942 11

1943 13

1944 15

1945 19

1946 31

1947 33

1948 37

1949 39

1950 47

Part II

Attic Treasures 57

December 11, 1945 The Exchange Club 63

1950-01-03 Cupid's Columns 122

Herman, 1940s Lonely Hearts Search, is the first book in the series. I can offer only a light sketch of my stepfather's early life because almost everyone is gone. Immigrant homesteaders didn't journal and take many pictures. They were busy tilling the earth and storing winter supplies for themselves and their livestock. Herman, a German immigrant's son, was representative of thousands of men searching for a wife after the Second World War. My goal is to introduce the reader to *one* returning veteran's struggle and the bleak fate so many unsuspecting women fell into.

In part II of this book, the historical significance of the singles catalogues— a window into the plight of thousands of women in post Second World War Two society—is linked to the lonely men searching for a wife. Maybe you'll find a relative, perhaps a mother, grandmother or great grandmother, among the hundreds of women who advertised themselves. I discovered my mother.

I have the cage. Now I need the bird.

Herman to Faye Monson, after he purchased the
family farm in 1946.
Faye, a 1930s Nebish, Minnesota, neighbor, told
me the story in 2016.

The "bird."

Author's mother, circa 1946.

From the Author

In an early version of this manuscript, I juxtaposed my mother and stepfather's lives through the 1940s. I came to realize that this first book is my stepfather's story because it was he who made first contact. In studying the lonely hearts catalogues hidden in the attic of our old farmhouse for decades, I imagined his anticipation when he began his search for a wife. As the search continued over months and years, despair and loneliness must have clouded his judgment. I tried to imagine his excitement when my mother, with four young children, stepped off the bus.

It's been more than seventy years since Herman Affield came home from WWII to his farm in northern Minnesota. It took him four years to find a woman. In his quest, he must have corresponded with many prospects. I think a few visited the farm—I know of one, other than my mother. I wonder what they saw in Herman that made them shy away. Was it Herman or was it the bleak farm, not much different from homesteader farms of the 1880s I read about as I researched his background?

The Affield family's American history is young: They were German immigrants who arrived in the 1890s. On the other hand, my mother's American history—and mine—began with the Olmsted brothers' arrival in Boston aboard the *Lyon* in1632—twelve years after the *Mayflower*, two-hundred-fifty years before the Affields. The Olmsted family name carried forward through my grandfather, Henry Olmsted Philips (1894-1957). My mother, all her life, considered herself a blue-blood aristocrat and a Daughter of the American Revolution.

I think as we grow older, we hope to find meaning in our life experience. With that in mind, since my stepfather initiated contact with my mother, I came to realize that to understand the dynamics that drove him to a singles catalogue, I needed to explore his history.

Prologue

Children raised in a dysfunctional home are not aware of the psychological forces they are dealing with. We all knew our mother was different but her behavior was our normal. My stepfather, Herman, was more normal but still, different. In the early 1990s I was diagnosed with post-traumatic stress disorder (PTSD), the result of combat in Vietnam during the late 1960s. I'm not a mental health specialist, but over the past twenty years of studying psychology, plus Herman's military records, I've come to realize he, too, lived with PTSD.

I was sixteen the spring of 1964 and tired of my parent's acrimony. My two older brothers had left the farm and I decided it was time for me to go. I spent much of the summer riding freight trains and living in hobo jungles in the Northwest. I look back from more than fifty years out and try to recall the men I met. They're faceless now, but I remember a story passed around in the Wenatchee jungle that prompted many of them to hop a freight car. Witnessing the way this story spread like wildfire, even through the prism of a teenager's worldview, I realized it was somehow unusual.

The tale circulated that there was a state program in the South—I don't recall what state—that was giving every homeless veteran fifty dollars, no residency requirement necessary. I don't know if it was true, but the story went that all one had to do was show up at the disbursement office with veteran identification.

Younger men gave older and crippled men a boost up into slow-rolling freights. I realize now, those old men were First World War veterans—possibly a Spanish American War veteran or two. The helpers, the majority of the hobos, were Second World War and Korean War veterans. How I wish I had known to take notes, to visit with those men.

Thomas Childers' book, *Soldier From The War Returning* (2009), explores the lives of *three* WWII veterans and their families. The book documents a part of our collective past—an inconvenient truth—that has been airbrushed from our national memory. Yet, like me and my siblings, millions of baby boomers grew up in the shadow of that history.

Statistics in the introduction of Childers' book grabbed my attention. He wrote: *By 1943 the U. S. Army was discharging ten thousand men each month for psychiatric reasons, and the numbers increased as the war dragged on. During the Battle of Okinawa...the Marines suffered twenty thousand psychiatric casualties. ...Veterans Administration (VA) hospitals were swamped with 'psychoneurotic' cases, and two years after the war's end, half the patients in the VA medical facilities were men suffering from 'invisible wounds.' Post-traumatic stress disorder (PTSD) was not diagnosed until 1980....* (page8).

Herman was one of those men who suffered "invisible wounds," one of the men who slipped through the cracks in 1948 when he sought help from an overwhelmed VA system.

The majority of hobos I lived with the summer of 1964 were no doubt a remnant of the legions of rootless veterans from those earlier conflicts. It was that summer I met my first Vietnam Veteran—of him my strongest memory is his drunken, unpredictable rages. Now I realize he was in the vanguard of my generation's invisible wound casualties.

Herman came of age in the 1920s and remained on the farm during the Great Depression except for short stints of working summers in Montana with his future brother-in-law, Charlie Hightshoe. When I asked Faye, Charlie's younger sister and a neighbor from the 1930s, why Herman didn't marry a local girl, she told me, "There was just no money to date. I liked him a lot and sent him letters when he was in the army, but he was just too much older than me." Several years ago, Herman's 101 year-old-sister, Elfrieda, told me, "Herman was very bashful."

As one year melted into the next during Herman's youth, I believe the isolation of working on the farm and Depression-era thriftiness contributed to his reticence. Herman's history is sketchy and I have relied heavily on his military records to reconstruct his story.

PART I

Effeld (Affield) Roots

Herman's early childhood can only be reconstructed from stories and extrapolating bits of surviving records. The Affield family's was a typical, early 20th century homesteading story of a German immigrant family searching for a better life than what the Old Country could offer.

Otto Effeld, sixteen years old, emigrated from Alt Jasnitz, West Prussia, to the United States in 1896. His older brother, Reinhold, took him in as a partner on Reinhold's farm, located in the fertile Red River Valley, in Wilkin County, east of Kent, Minnesota. Both young men had left Europe before they were seventeen to avoid conscription into the German Army.

The summer of 1904, as a junior partner, Otto was employed by his brother and wife. In 1905, he returned to West Prussia and eloped with his childhood sweetheart.

Otto Effeld and Bertha Sonnenberg, 1905 wedding portrait.
Wahpeton, North Dakota.

(At some point, the last name was Americanized to Affield.)
(Courtesy of Elfrieda LaDaux family collection.)

My stepfather was born on April 6, 1906, in Wahpeton, North Dakota, the eldest of five children. He was baptized, Herman Arthur Effeld, in a German Lutheran Church on July 29, 1906.

Documents show that Otto and his young family moved a few times. First to Pengilly, Minnesota, then back to Kent, where Otto again worked for a time with his brother. I'm not sure exactly when Otto and Bertha moved to Nebish, Minnesota. From surviving documents and records I believe they first arrived there about 1910.

"Nebish" is derived from the Ojibwe-language word "tea." According to *Red Lake Nation, Portraits of Ojibway Life,* by Charles Brill, the first Europeans reached the Red Lake area—including Nebish—in 1798 (page 25). Less than one hundred years later, immigrant loggers arrived. Between 1885 and 1930, millions of board feet of lumber were shipped out of Nebish and the surrounding region by rail; some logs were floated out on Mud River. Most of the logging was done in the winter when the ground was frozen so horse teams could skid out clean logs. There were other reasons logging was a winter occupation. Mosquitoes, horse flies, and deer flies were unbearable in the summer forests. Also, many of the loggers had farm homesteads they worked from spring breakup through autumn harvest.

It must have been a winter in the mid-1950s, when Otto came to visit us in Nebish. Wrapped in an old quilt, he sat in the front room kitchen, visiting with my mother. His thick accent fascinated me. Otto, the logger—he loved to talk about the old days. One story that stuck in my mind was of how, during Holy Communion, the Lutheran loggers knelt piously waiting for the chalice. When it was passed, they sipped, dipped their beards, passed the cup, and went back to their pew and sucked the Blood from their beards. Maybe Otto witnessed the event. Maybe he dipped his beard. I'm sure not all did it, maybe a few, but the story became a part of his logger lore.

Otto was a tough taskmaster to his children. Besides winter logging, he worked on the railroad in the summer. He must have been gone a fair amount of time, forcing added responsibility on his wife and young children. I wonder if German was spoken in the home because Herman, throughout his life, slurred certain consonants and vowels.

"Hermy [Herman], Me [Elfrieda], and Bruno Affield," reads the caption below the earliest photo, circa 1914. (Caption written many years later.) It's a professional setting at a studio in Wahpeton, N.D. Bruno is 4 years old; Hermy, 9; Elfrieda, 8.

Ervin and Stella are not yet born.
(Courtesy of Elfrieda LaDaux family collection.)

The fact that this photo was taken in Wahpeton is one of the time gaps I don't understand. If Otto and Bertha had a homestead in Nebish, what were they doing in Wahpeton? Who was taking care of their livestock?

Bruno Effeld's headstone in the Nebish Community Cemetery is dated August 28, 1915, within a year of when this picture was taken.

Bertha and a neighbor lady were traveling to visit an ailing friend. Bruno, sitting on the back of the buckboard and no doubt swinging his feet, was thrown from the buckboard and killed when one of the first automobiles in the Nebish area spooked the horse. Faye Monson verified that Bertha was also thrown, slammed her head against a tree, and suffered a traumatic brain injury. For the rest of her life she suffered seizures. At that time, there were no seizure medications. A family member had to be with Bertha at all times. I heard one story that she fell against the hot wood cook stove and was seriously burned.

Old Nebish was built on the northeast side of Nebish Lake less than a mile from the Affield homestead. The town was abandoned in 1908 in favor of the new and current Nebish town site, about one mile east. I imagine Herman and his brother, Ervin, spent many hours exploring the abandoned buildings when they were children. As kids in the 1950s, Randy and I walked from the farm to Nebish Store, searching the ditches for long neck beer bottles and an occasional pop bottle— good for three cents and two cents, respectively. But we'd cut across the neighbor's pasture, eliminating a big "U" in the road. The shortcut took us across the Old Nebish town site and we'd kick up bricks and bits of rusted metal each time we trespassed.

To better understand Herman's childhood I gleaned some information about early Nebish from *The Red Lake Line, A Railroad Built in the Wilderness,* by William and Madeline Sutherland (2008). It's a collection of documented stories and oral histories of our area.

Florence Edwards Gilman was the local news reporter for many years and the Nebish School cafeteria manager my first few years in school. In the 1970s, Florence interviewed our Uncle Charlie Hightshoe. Charlie married Herman's youngest sister, Stella, in 1942. In the interview with Mrs. Gilman, Charlie talked about what happened to the buildings at Old Nebish: "Nebish had two schools, one at Old Nebish and the other over a couple of miles on the old Leech Lake Trail, going to Red Lake. My wife's folks [Otto and Bertha Affield] bought the old school building at Old Nebish and it still stands, just a mile south of here, but it has been built onto."

That was the home Herman was raised in, and the home I would live in two decades later. In the dead of winter, the schoolhouse was skidded across the lake to the Affield homestead and placed on a foundation with a dirt floor basement. The following summer a two story addition was built on the east side of the house and an upstairs added to the schoolhouse section.

Old Nebish School, circa 1898. Otto Affield moved the building to the Affield homestead. Courtesy of Beltrami County History Center.

I believe that Otto salvaged other buildings from Old Nebish. In a written history, *Old Nebish and Other Towns On the Red Lake Line,* Andrew Bergquist wrote, "When I first came to Nebish [autumn, 1904] there was an old blacksmith shop built of logs..." (page 2). We had a log blacksmith shop on the farm—it still stands. The roof is solid but the bottom and corners are rotting. My oldest brother, Chris, recalls a note scratched into a log near the forge that fascinated him when he was a little boy, "Clinton Larsen, big-assed Swede." To my knowledge, no Swedes ever lived on the Affield homestead.

And there's another building—low, long. From a black and white photo of Old Nebish, it appears to have rough-cut board siding and looks very similar to the barn we had on the homestead when my mother and we four children first arrived at the farm in 1949. In the 1930s, the original Affield barn was struck by lightning and burned. It was the Great Depression. Did the Affield family salvage the abandoned building from Old Nebish, disassemble it, reconstruct it on the homestead, and use it as a dairy barn for the next fifteen years?

Like so much of history, the Sutherland collection airbrushed out a portion of local history. Many years ago I was riding the VFW van to the Fargo VA Hospital for some forgotten reason. The van left Bemidji about 6:00 A.M. for the three-hour trip. Midway over, as we passed by a collection of abandoned and collapsing shacks, one of the passengers, a WWII veteran, recalled how, when he was a kid, there was a whorehouse in that little railroad/logging town. I had wondered how the Nebish loggers and railroad workers were entertained. The Sutherland account does mention that there were, "...two saloons a little north of the town...." (page 8).

One street in new Nebish my brothers and I loved to weave into conversation was Pig Turd Alley. There's no assonance or consonance, but in the mind there's certain imagery because of the incongruity. Originally, there had been a small pig farm on the trail, but by the time new Nebish matured, the farm was a poetic memory. By 1920 there was a nondenominational chapel at one end of the trail and a railroad station where the pig pen had been. After the timber was gone, the rails were ripped out and the station was converted to a home with a large screen porch.

Across from the house was a three-acre diamond willow swamp that filled with melt water each spring. It's still there. The new school was on the other side of the swamp. It's still there too, though closed and boarded up since 1962. By the time my younger brother, Randy, and I walked the ditches to Nebish in the 1950s, the house on Pig Turd Alley was abandoned, only lived in for a few weeks each spring by the Grip family, an itinerant sheep shearer, his wife and several children. Even though we had explored it countless times, "Let's go visit the Grip house on Pig Turd Alley," was all it took to set Randy and me on our way.

There were several abandoned tarpaper shacks with dirt floors in the new Nebish suburbs. By the 1950s they were rotting into the ground. But in the early days, loggers lived in them, some with families.

Several years ago my wife, Patti, and I went to visit Elfrieda, the little girl in the picture, just before her 102nd birthday. She told me that she left home to work in a boarding house at fourteen so didn't recall much about life on the Affield homestead. I asked her about a story we had grown up with.

As children, we slept in the unheated upstairs of the old farmhouse. For years, Randy and I snuggled under a stiff horsehide robe fringed with a tattered green felt strip. I remember how, in the darkness, I would finger the bristle-covered holes in one section of the course blanket.

Charlie Hightshoe told the story that Herman and his brother, Ervin, had been trying to catch a stallion to harness for work. In a fit of rage Herman flung a pitchfork at the stallion and the tines pierced the horse's stomach. Otto beat Herman—beat him badly—and made him skin the horse, flesh the hide, and tan it. Herman slept beneath the robe until he left for the army. Charlie said they ate the horse.

When I asked 102-year-old Elfrieda about the story, she said, "Oooh, that was bad." She hesitated, looked at me, shook her head and said, "I don't remember that." I wonder if Herman's act was a child's fit of anger, perhaps lashing out at the horse that had bolted when Bruno was killed.

Herman Affield, Circa 1935

I recall another story that Charlie related. During the Great Depression of the 1930s, Herman and he worked on a ranch in Montana. One weekend they went into a town, and Herman told Charlie to look at the *sheep*.

Charlie looked about, and said, "Where? I don't see any sheep."

"Right there. The sheep, across the street. The red sheep."

"That's a Jeep, not a sheep," Charlie informed him. As I mentioned earlier, Herman slurred his consonants. But by 1940 the Affield family was assimilated into the American way of life and they all spoke English.

I wonder what Otto and Bertha thought as Hitler and the German government moved toward war in the mid 1930s. Did they feel an allegiance to the old country? Did the family—through three-day-old newspapers—follow Germany's conquest of Austria on March 1, 1938? When Hitler bullied his way into Czechoslovakia, were the American Affields happy or concerned? And on September 1, 1939, when the German Wehrmacht (military) invaded Poland where the European Affield family lived, along with millions of other Germans, were they worried? (Little could they know that my mother, a music student studying abroad, and Herman's future wife, escaped Poland and the invasion five days before it began.)

When Otto's sons were drafted into the U.S. army in 1942, what advice might he have given them? I wonder who left first, Ervin, who served in the Pacific against the Japanese, or Herman, who shipped to the European Theater. What did the brothers discuss as they parked their vehicles in the garage and blocked them up so the tires wouldn't rot while they were gone? Did they tell each other they could have their car if they didn't return? Did Herman wonder if any of his first cousins wore the German uniform?

As I mentioned earlier, the European Affield family roots were in Alt Jasnitz, West Prussia, about ninety miles south of Danzig, near the Polish Corridor which bordered the Baltic Sea. During WWII that area was hotly contested between Polish Resistance fighters and Hitler's German Army. In the end, the Russian Army was in control and would be for the next fifty years. In 1945, surviving Polish-German people—families who had lived in Poland for centuries—were ostracized and forced to relocate to Germany.

The *Reinhold Affield Family* book states that after 1938 there was no longer communication with the European Affields. Today, if you were to mail a letter to Alt Jasnitz, it would be sent to Stary Jasinec, Poland. Steve Affield and his family have returned to the Old Country homestead twice. He told me that after Germany was defeated in WWII, and all residents of German heritage were banished from West Prussia, German family cemetery plots were left to grow over. Are there any Affield (Effeld) descendants in Germany or Poland today?

1942

On April 20, 1942, four months after Japan bombed Pearl Harbor and the U.S. declaration of war on Japan and Germany, two days after the Doolittle Raid on Tokyo, Herman, thirty-six years old, was inducted into the army at Fort Snelling, Minnesota. According to his military record, he had blue eyes and brown hair and was quite stocky, 5' 5.5" and 190 pounds. His civilian occupation was listed as "Farmer, general." His military occupational specialty: "Carpenter, general." In the army, he was trained as a Combat Infantryman. On July 1, 1942, he filled out a Defense Savings Bond Application, with his sister, Stella, as co-owner. The war bonds were sent home to Nebish for safekeeping.

After seven months of training—including amphibious assault training—Herman departed the United States on October 24, 1942, in a convoy consisting of 105 ships. His troop convoy steamed directly from the U.S. to the landing beaches of the North African invasion. Records show that he arrived on November 8, 1942, and received a 20 percent raise for foreign service.

I remember the first ship I was sent to after recruit training in 1965. When it got underway from San Diego, we were barely beyond the harbor mouth when I started getting queasy. There was nowhere on the ship to escape the constant motion—the pitch and roll of the ship. After four days of training maneuvers in the Pacific, we pulled into San Francisco Bay. As soon as we moored, I was lowered on a scaffold to scrub my crusted vomit off the haze gray sides of the destroyer.

I wonder if Herman got seasick. Troopships were notoriously over-crowded. It's not hard to visualize this Midwestern farmer who had grown up with his feet firmly planted on solid ground, packed in with thousands of other troops, eating greasy food, the air permeated with body odor and stale cigarette smoke, confined to berthing compartments because the ocean was so rough, the smell of others regurgitating. After fifteen days of that, how combat-ready were these men when they were ordered over the side of the ship to the landing craft for the assault on November 8, the day they arrived? My guess is, they were happy to go.

Operation Torch consisted of three Groups; the Western Task For-ce—which I believe Herman was in—landed on the Atlantic shores of French Morocco with beaches at Safi, Casablanca, and Mehdia. The Center and Eastern Task Forces landed on the more protected beaches of the Mediterranean, at Oran and the Algiers, respectively. WWII ships' movement reports reveal that the Western Task Force departed Norfolk, Virginia, on October 24-25, 1942—the same day Herman de-parted the U.S.

Herman participated in the first U.S. amphibious landings of the war. During the Western Task Force's initial assault in the high Atlantic surf, sixty landing craft were swamped—filled with water and sank—with he-avy loss of life. The landings were nothing compared to the bloody Nor-mandy landings three years later. In North Africa, the Vichy French and Italians did put up resistance but were quickly defeated. Within days, the French capitulated and began fighting on the Allies' side.

1943

On January 14, 1943, President Franklin Delano Roosevelt (FDR) flew to Morocco to meet secretly with British Prime Minister Churchill and French representatives (Allies) to plot a strategy to victory in WWII. Security must have been incredible. I don't recall Herman ever talking about the Casablanca Conference, January 14-24, 1943, but I imagine, as a private first class (PFC), he was not privy to knowledge beyond the next sand dune.

By February the Allies had pushed the German and Italian armies east along the Mediterranean Coast to Kasserine Pass, where the German Army made a stand in a series of desperate battles. Herman must have participated in that campaign and continued east in pursuit. His discharge—DD214—shows that he received a Combat Infantryman Award on 25 May 1943.

According to a 1948 Veterans Administration (VA) report, *In Africa [Herman] was pulled back [from the front lines] for a rest and re-examined before being returned to the front. This was 1943. Blood pressure was found higher than normal and he was taken out of combat.*

Herman was transferred from North Africa to Great Britain. His VA report continued… *He lay around in a replacement depot and then went to work in a post office. He sat down at this job all the time.*

1944

On June 3, 1944, two days before the D-Day landings at Normandy, Herman left Great Britain, enroute to the United States. He arrived in the U.S. on June 14. His VA report states that, "In the United States, after a 24-day delay during which time he went home, he was examined at Camp Butler, N.C."

June 1944, Nebish, Minnesota, farm. Family members pose with Herman, (far left) who is thirty-eight years old, after he returned from combat in North Africa.

I imagine Herman, drowsy and bewildered, getting off the train in Bemidji, after being gone for two years. Was anyone there to meet him? I remember when I came home from Vietnam, I got off the bus and no one was there. I recall how I felt—kind of at a loss as I hitchhiked the twenty miles out to the farm.

On June 19, 1944, while Herman was on leave, he was listed on "Battle Casualty or Rotational Extract." Victory in Europe (VE) was proclaimed almost a year later on May 8, 1945. After VE Day, it took almost two years to bring all the troops home.

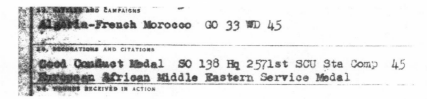

According to Herman's DD 214, he received a Battle and Campaign ribbon for the Algeria-French Morocco campaign. He also received a Good Conduct Medal and the European African Middle Eastern Service Medal. (Awarded to all troops who served in one or all of the noted campaigns.) In the bottom box, Wounds Received in Action, it says "None."

Herman's 1948 VA medical report stated that, *He doesn't know what his blood pressure was then [in 1944]. He was separated at Fort Belvore, Virginia. He put in a claim for hypertension and in 3 or 4 months the checks started coming. So far he has had no examination by or for the VA.*

I sometimes visit with my oldest brother, Chris, picking his mind about our early years on the farm. He recalled a story that Herman told about a morning formation in North Africa when he shot an Arab civilian who was loitering near the American troops. Herman's company commander told him he was in trouble until Herman opened the blanket the Arab had draped over his shoulders and removed a knife and a 9mm German Luger. Chris also recalled that Herman was the oldest man in his unit—other G.I.s called him "Pops."

Perhaps the tale that left the most lasting impression on me as a young boy was how Arabs of North Africa, employed by the German Army, would cut the tent walls or slither beneath them in the desert sand, into sleeping American soldiers' tents at night, slit a soldier's throat, and then slice off his ears. The Germans paid a bounty on fresh ears.

I can still remember Herman's calloused cow-smelling hands, how he grabbed my ears and sliced with an imaginary knife.

1945

Herman Affield at Fort Belvore 1945

From mid-1944 well into 1945, Herman was stationed at Fort Belvore, Virginia, in an army holding company, assigned to menial tasks such as working in the kitchen. Peeling potatoes must have been a touchstone of that time. When we were kids we'd sit around a slop bucket in the kitchen peeling potatoes with our little jackknives. Herman always made it a contest with my younger brother, Randy, and me to see who could make the longest, thinnest peel before it broke and fell in the pail. Herman often repeated his army stories about working in the kitchen—of how, "I'd go to the kitchen at two in the morning to peel spuds for breakfast—two hundred pounds." Herman pronounced spuds, "shpudsh".

I wonder if May 8, 1945, Victory in Europe (VE Day), was a depressing time for Herman. Did he reflect on the fate of the men he had fought beside in North Africa? Survivor guilt is a universal burden for those who leave the battlefield early, leave their friends behind. I remember after I was medevaced home from Vietnam, at night on the hospital ward we sometimes wondered to each other what happened to those left behind. Did Herman feel guilt about leaving early? Or did he just feel his war was over and he wanted to go home to the farm.

On June 9, 1945, he requested a discharge for dependency—a hardship discharge—to help out on the farm in Nebish. A member of the Beltrami County Selective Service Board requested the Welfare Board to do an evaluation of the Affield family.

Medical Field Agent
Beltrami County Welfare Board
Bemidji, Minnesota

Re: Herman A. Affield
ASN: 37 268 232

Dear Sir:

The above named registrant of our Board is requesting discharge from the Army by reason of dependency.

Will you kindly make an investigation based on the grounds of extreme hardship and privation of the dependents, and give us a report that we may submit to our State Headquarters that will aid them in making a decision.

The parents of this man are living in Nebish, Minnesota.

Yours very truly,

Marlyce Bergsven

Marlyce Bergsven, Clerk
Beltrami County Local Board

MB:mg

FIELD AGENT'S REPORT:

Affield, Herman A. 06-15-45. On this date the worker made an investigation as requested by the Selective Service Board. It was found that the location to the Otto Affield farm is as follows: (Otto Affield is the natural father of Herman A. Affield). Go north on Irvine Avenue past Lake Julia Sanitarium near Puposky. Just past the Sanitarium will be noted a prominent corner where there is a closed filling station. Proceed straight north on CAR#15 about two and one half miles where #15 turns right. Proceed north about four miles on the main road until a lake will be noticed ahead. Just before reaching the lake will be observed a white house with a red barn on the right. This is the home of the Affields.

Before arriving at the farm, the worker contacted a reliable collateral who knew something regarding the Affield situation. This collateral informed the worker that Mr. and Mrs. Otto Affield are the only occupants of the farm home. Further discussion disclosed the fact that Mrs. Affield is suffering from some type of "fits" and Mr. Affield is the only one in the home to care for her. This retards Mr. Affield's ability to work the farm but the collateral was under the impression that most of the farm was worked on a share basis. It seems that several years ago a daughter was in the home and could assist with the care of the mother. Since that time, this daughter has married and is now Mrs. Charles Hightshoe and the Hightshoe's now have three children. It is impossible for Mrs. Hightshoe to offer her services to her mother. It was further learned that Herman Affield has 80 acres of land adjoining his father's farm on which there are no buildings. Previous to his induction in the Army, Herman always lived at the home and assisted his father and mother in running the farm.

This collateral also made the following remark during the course of conversation: "I was always under the impression that Otto Affield was pretty well fixed." This remark was made since the worker purposely withheld the basic reason for her investigation. The worker then proceeded to the Affield home and found no one there. It was observed that the home was moderately good, rather large farm structure in a fair state of repair. There were two garages on the place and one garage door was open leading one to suppose that a car had recently been driven out. Next to this empty stall was a Plymouth Coupe which was up on blocks and was presumably not used.

This Plymouth was about a 1936 Model with a 1942 license plate on it. This car presumably belongs to Herman Affield, now in the United States Army, and would have a present sale value of about $250.00. The second garage, which was open, housed a 1941 Chevrolet Couch which was practically new. This car had a 1945 license number on it and it was noted through the car window that the mileage was 38,000 miles. This Chevrolet is worth approximately $800.00 or $900.00 at the present sale price. The Chevrolet Coach presumably belongs to Ervin Affield, brother of Herman Affield who is also in the United States Army.

A third car was observed by the worker standing next to the Chevrolet Coach which was an old Pontiac with 59,000 miles on it and a 1942 license plate. This car was in running order with three good tires and would probably sell at about $100.00 or slightly less at the present time. It is therefore assumed by the worker that since the family has four cars, two of which are being used at the present time, that the Affield financial straits is not desperate.

A separate shed housed a fairly new tractor and in the yard were several pieces of practically new farm equipment made by Allis Chalmers. Several head of cattle were grazing in a nearby field and since the barn door was open these animals no doubt belonged to the Affields.

Since the Affields were not home and since a personal conversation could not be had with them the worker then contacted their nearest neighbor, and secured the following information.

The second collateral said that Mrs. Affield has had epileptic fits for the past ten years. He did not believe that she was under the care of a doctor at the present time since little can be done for her condition. This collateral felt that Otto Affield was fairly well off financially. This man also quoted that the Affields had tried to keep Herman out of the

Army since the beginning and he felt that Herman was not needed on the farm any more than thousands of other boys who are also needed. This second collateral disclosed the fact that he, himself, had two sons in the forces of the United States. He said that he, too, could very easily use his boys on the farm but was managing to struggle along without them.

The worker feels that in view of Mrs. Affield's poor health status that Herman could be of material benefit to his parents. However, from a standpoint of privation of dependents the worker feels that such privation does not exist. Observation of the cars owned by the family, the better than average farm home, and the ownership of livestock are factors taken into consideration by the worker.

A copy of this case recording will be sent to the Selective Service Office.

Date Dict. 6-16-45   Grace K. Olson
Date Tran. 6-20-45   Social Worker-a

.50 Caliber ammunition box Herman brought home from WWII. In it, he stored important papers including the lonely hearts club catalogues I found.

On October 8, 1945, Herman received an Honorable Discharge. Ten years older than the average soldier, he was a conscientious, reliable trooper who performed his duty when his country called upon him. He returned to the farm with a dream and a gray .50 caliber ammunition box filled with military memories. I remember the day I was discharged from the Navy in 1969. I felt empty, at loose ends after four years of military discipline, melancholy yet very happy to be free, proud that I had served honorably. I imagine Herman felt all those things. He was probably eager to get home and help get the farm tucked in for winter.

In *Nebish History and Memories*, published in 2000, I found this information about Herman that had been written in the *Northland Times*, a small newspaper published in Bemidji.

October 19, 1945—Herman Affield arrived home Thursday and has been honorably discharged. He served in Africa, Sicily, and Italy while in the service. He entered the Armed Forces in April 1942, so has spent over three years in the service.

Military discharge papers are notorious for being inaccurate. According to VA records, he was pulled from the front before the Sicily and Italy invasions. When we were children, he never mentioned those later operations, so I believe the write-up is not correct. Perhaps it was written that way because the European African Middle Eastern Service Medal was awarded for one or all campaigns, but as noted earlier, he received a Battle and Campaign ribbon only for the Algeria-French Morocco campaign.

December 11, 1945, home on the farm, Herman gave himself an early Christmas gift—a lonely hearts club catalogue, *The Exchange Club*, Kansas City, Missouri. As I mentioned earlier, Herman's sister told me that he was very shy. The back page of this catalogue sounds like what he needed.

DEVOTED TO THE INTERESTS OF THE UNMARRIED

The Exchange

No. 344

PUBLISHED BY THE

EXCHANGE CLUB KANSAS CITY, MO.

3827 Main Street, Kansas City, Mo.
Established in 1909

(Full text in Part II)

You say you are too shy, don't know how to go about it, are not sure it's "the right thing to do." As far as being shy is concerned, meeting people through friendly letters is easier than meeting them in person— you learn to know them slowly and easily, and take your time getting used to them between letters. And it's such fun to get letters.

The faded blue catalogue with the girl holding a parasol is folded in half and worn. When first discovered, it had a thin string tied around with the folded "key" of names and addresses safely secured. When I untied it, I remember thinking that Herman, forty years dead, had tied the knot in the late 1940s.

He probably carried the catalogue in his back pocket while working and pulled it out to study whenever he paused for a break. Many pages have margin notes with the woman's address. I imagine him sitting in the kitchen of the old farmhouse in the glow of a kerosene lantern, twilight deepening at the end of a long day working alone, dreaming of a wife and children.

Herman, circa 1946. Is this the photo he sent to women?

Maybe after spending the past three years with other people, Herman realized he was lonely. Perhaps seeing combat made him conscious of his mortality. I remember when I returned from Vietnam and rushed into a marriage. How excited I was when my son was born—how much I loved to play on the floor with him and later, when he could walk, go to the park with him. But marriage requires more than that. In retrospect, I was not prepared—knew nothing about the responsibilities. Within a few years the marriage was a failure. Herman, like me, was very naive in his ideas of what marriage would entail.

I think now, he and I shared a very similar experience. We had been raised in the isolation of rural northern Minnesota, left home and participated in a life-altering experience, and returned home several years older to a civilian society that we knew nothing about.

WWII resulted in the widowhood of thousands of women. A whole new generation of single women—war time high school graduates— were also trying to find their place in life. Add to that chaos, millions of returning men and women, veterans of the most violent war in history, searching for a new normal. It was a time of upheaval as Herman set out on his quest. The two dollars he paid for the "key"—the list of names and addresses of the women in the catalogue—included a twelve-month membership in *The Exchange*.

I suspect he agonized over spending the two dollars and studied the catalogue while he waited for the address list. I imagine he recorded the numbers of the women who caught his eye, so when the key did arrive, he was ready to put a name and address to each listing.

In this first catalogue Herman received, he wrote the addresses of twenty-three women in the page margins. Did he contact them all? It's hard to imagine what went through his mind as he fantasized about life with each woman. The first one in the book had grabbed his attention, and he recorded her name and address. Where did his imagination take him?

MAKE YOUR OWN SELECTIONS

Two Dollars pays for the name and address of every lady given in this Catalogue. You make the selections yourself from this list of descriptions. The published descriptions contain full information in regard to the ladies, their age, religion, personal appearance, means, value of property, etc.

The original descriptions are always on file in our office. The full names and addresses of the ladies will be sent you by return mail in a plain envelope on receipt of $2.00. Send your orders now and be one of the first to correspond.

3—I make a good appearance, dress reasonably well but not extravagantly, and try to adjust myself in a reasonable way, concerning most things. My specialty is my home and its environments, cooking, planning meals, etc. American, Presbyterian, high school and business college education, secretary, age 35, chestnut brown hair, blue-grey eyes, fair complexion, ht. 5-3, wt. 106. Worth $4000.

4—I am a widow by death, like sports, dancing, good music, a nice home, flowers and pets, like to play cards and entertain. Have a nice appearance, dress neatly, fair looking. German, Catholic, common school education, age 52, light brown hair, blue eyes, fair complexion, ht. 5-5, wt. 120. Own home and car. Interested in someone congenial, 55 to 60.

5—Have always been considered very neat and stylish in appearance. I enjoy traveling, camping and fishing, also like a good show. Irish-American, Methodist, college educated, age 59, light hair, blue eyes, fair complexion, ht. 5-5, wt. 145. Own property and oil interests. Would like to hear from a gentleman 60 to 70.

1—Considered very attractive, a neat dresser, have a quiet disposition, easy to get along with. Am a good cook and housekeeper. My favorite sports are bowling, horseback riding and dancing. Have some talent in music, play a guitar. English, Christian, common school education, age 20, dark hair, blue eyes, fair complexion, ht. 5-7, wt. 122. See my photo above.

6—I am friendly and jolly, like sports, fond of country life. My friends

Most of the women who attracted Herman's attention were in their mid-thirties, which makes sense; a few were teenagers. Number 1, Myrtis M. Wolfer, PO Box 127, Honey Island, Texas, loved to dance and party, very unlike Herman. What attracted him? She had sound credentials but was about half his age.

81—Considered a very nice girl, have lots of friends, no bad habits, keep good company, also a good Christian, fair education, farmer girl, age 18, dark brown hair, brown eyes, fair complexion, ht. 5-5, wt. 116, slender figure. Would like to correspond with a young man of fair education, one in business, or one that likes farm life. See my photo above.

althea Hughes Sams valle
RI.
marietta akla

And what about number 81—a teenager? Today, in our materialistic society, it's hard to imagine what a young woman, who came of age during the war years, a young woman who spent her childhood in the Depression, expected from life. What dreams might this teenager who was raised on an Oklahoma farm have? Did she come from a prosperous farm or did she come from a hardscrabble family of Joads—Steinbeck's Dustbowl creation from *The Grapes of Wrath*?

32—I have a good, honest name, and can give best of reference. I have a very pleasing disposition, considered nice looking. Farmerette, fair education, age 32, brown hair, blue eyes, fair complexion, ht. 4-10, wt. 159. I own a good farm with good buildings, also a store on highway. Would like to hear from a gentleman 35 to 40, a good worker.

Mrs. Alma Callahan
Turkey Ky.

Number 32 is a curiosity; did Herman consider selling his farm and relocating to hers?

There are no surviving letter drafts that he wrote to women. I believe he sent the original draft with a word or phrase crossed out or overwritten. I would love to know how he presented himself. For a man with an eighth grade education he was quite articulate and reasonably versed in grammar.

Did Herman make a list of qualities he wanted in a mate? From his mindset in the 1950s when I was a child, I'm sure Catholics were ruled out. Or did he cast a wide net, curious at what kind of responses he would receive?

I don't think Herman had a very positive self-image. His bashfulness revealed itself quite early. Visiting with Herman's old friend, Faye, I got a glimpse of Herman as a young man. Faye was twenty years younger than Charlie and Herman so recalls from a young girl's point of view. She told me that Herman sometimes worked for Charlie in the 1920s and 30s. At the end of the week, Charlie asked Herman how much he owed him in wages. Faye told me, "Herman hung his head, too bashful to set a price, letting Charlie figure it out." She continued on, "Herman was playful, like a big brother. Sometimes he'd sneak up and pull my ponytail."

As I think back, Herman was always subservient to other men. I remember how, when hog or cattle buyers came to the farm, they always controlled the conversation. When Herman sold the dairy herd in the late 1960s, one buyer quoted him a price; the next day a second buyer offered him a higher price, so Herman naturally went with him. The first buyer came back, angry because he had lost a sale and demanded that Herman give him a free cow. Herman did.

1946

The Best Years of Our Lives, a movie that explored postwar readjustment of returning men, was released in 1946. The country was aware of psychological and social undercurrents as a result of the war, but millions of men didn't understand the psychological load they brought home, and women, especially in rural and underdeveloped areas, had no idea of why their fathers, brothers, husbands, and boy friends were withdrawn, jumpy, angry. Why so many turned to alcohol.

On June 11, 1946, eight months after Herman was discharged from the army, he purchased the farm from his parents. The deed reads, for "$1 and other good and valuable considerations." During one of my visits with Elfrieda, I asked her why Herman ended up with the farm for one dollar. She explained that Otto had cashed and spent the savings bonds Herman sent home while he was in the army. A few months after he purchased the farm, Otto and Bertha moved to Pengilly, the area where they had attempted to homestead more than thirty years earlier.

Was Herman too difficult to live with? Childers wrote in his well-researched book, ...*in the aftermath of the Second World War, depression, recurring nightmares, survivor guilt, outbursts of rage (most frequently directed at family members), exaggerated startle responses, and anxiety reactions—all of which are recognized today as classic symptoms of PTSD—were as common as they were unnerving. ...many veterans simply suffered in private— often with devastating consequences for them and their families* (page 8). Was this the temperament of the man, still beyond the horizon, my mother was on a collision course with—

the man she attempted to escape from two years after she married him?

During 1946, alone on his farm, Herman received several bulletins from *The Exchange*. I wonder if he attempted to contact any of these new names. These updated bulletins advertised new clients.

THE EXCHANGE
3827 Main St.,
Kansas City, Mo.

1-Miss Clyde Simmons, 501 Preusser St., San Angelo, Texas. Very happy disposition, considerate of others. Considered very neat appearing, wear nice clothes. Scotch-Irish, Baptist, well educated, a nurse, age 38, dark brown hair, grey eyes, olive complexion, ht 5-7½, wt 147. Interested in one near my age, with at least moderate means.
2-Mildred Zuke, 7 - 15th St. N. E. Mason City, Iowa. I am jolly, full of fun, like a good time. Considered neat and attractive. American, Lutheran, fair education, beauty operator, age 31, dark brown hair, hazel eyes, medium fair, ht 5-6, wt 140.
3-Mrs. M. J. Palmer, Box 513, Robert Lee, Texas. I love to keep house, cook and garde. have a pretty yard. Considered fair looking. American, Methodist, age 63, dark slightly grey hair, brown eyes, ht 5-2, wt 142. Desire neat appearing companion, good character

In August, 1946, Herman ordered a new lonely hearts club catalogue: *Standard Correspondence Club*. It arrived in a plain brown manila envelope accompanied by pages of late-signed clients and testimonials. The identification key for this next catalogue has been lost or perhaps Herman didn't see any women who interested him enough to pay the extra two dollars.

Standard Correspondence Club

Devoted to the interests of the unmarried.

T.M. Reg. U.S. Pat Off.

1   *J. W. Schlosser, Founder, Ella Schlosser Davis, Publisher and Editor, Grayslake, Illinois*

Reliable and Satisfactory Dealings
t, Legitimate Enterprise   AUGUST, 1946   Patronized by Some of the
Business Sacredly

1947

Even before WWII ended, Communist Dictator Joseph Stalin maneuvered to expand and consolidate conquered territory. In a 1946 speech, Winston Churchill referred to the imaginary boundary between communist controlled Eastern Europe and free Europe as the Iron Curtain. The world knew the Soviets were developing an atomic bomb. On August 29, 1949, they conducted their first successful test and thus became the second nation to have a nuclear bomb. Soviet expansion into Asia and the Korean Peninsula intensified tensions. Herman must have been aware of these developments but knew he would never again be drafted. It was against this backdrop that he expanded his search.

He must have been impressed with *Standard Correspondence Club* because he purchased the $5.00 Special soon after the new year. Northern Minnesota winters, especially in the late 1940s, were very isolating. I recall as a child in the 1950s, our quarter-mile-long driveway was drifted closed for more than a week at times. Herman shoveled it by hand, one end often drifted closed again by the time he reached the township road. During those solitary hours in the 1940s, as he scooped shovels of snow, he must have thought about women he had written to.

I can only imagine his loneliness during the heart of the winter. I wonder if that desolation is what prompted him to invest two weeks' cream income on the "Certificate of Service."

Certificate of Service

38

No. 012047
111447

$ 2.00
3.00

Do not lose this Certificate.
Without it you cannot get service

This is to Certify that

Herman Affield,

Box 7, Nebish, Minn.

Is entitled to services until married or one year from date of
issue, Feb 20, 1947 .... At any time the person whose
name appears above desires a new list of lady correspondents,
send us this certificate with 10 cents to defray the cost of postage, printing and stationery. We will return it to you with a
list of ladies who have recently requested gentlemen correspondents of suitable age; also the current issue with addresses and
introductions.

THIS CERTIFICATE EXPIRES when married.

Note the Box 7: Rural mail delivery didn't reach our area until the mid -1950s. I recall riding on the Farmall tractor with Herman as he drove two miles into Nebish for the mail. I try to imagine his anticipation in the late 1940s, as he drove in to pick up his mail.

Herman's 1948 VA medical report reads, *During the past year [1947, Herman] has had frontal headaches. His eyes smart on reading. He sleeps well after midnight and gets up at 6:30 with help of an alarm clock. No nocturia and no urinary trouble. No glasses. If he hurries in his work his heart beats hard and fast. Is on a farm by himself and milks 3 cows now but has seven. He has a tractor and good equipment —otherwise he couldn't keep up on the farm. Weight in the army was 195. (This report shows he weighs 165).*

I wonder if part of Herman's stress came from his yearning for a family. Headaches are common in PTSD sufferers. Sleep disturbance and nightmares are hallmarks of PTSD. Heart palpitations and isolation, eating disorders and weight loss—all might be PTSD symptoms. Did his longing, his feeling of emptiness, exacerbate his PTSD symptoms?

```
Award      25 May 43
        APPLICATION FOR
  READJUSTMENT ALLOWANCE
        PUBLIC LAW # 346
  MADE THROUGH
  STATE          MINNESOTA
  DATE    12-12-45
```

Originally, the G.I. Bill was called the Serviceman's Readjustment Act (Public Law 78-346). I found this stamped on Herman's discharge papers.

After the war Herman drove into Bemidji with his neighbor, Karl Knutson, and attended agricultural classes on the G.I. Bill. A few years ago Karl, a WWII veteran, shared the following story told by Herman while they drove to class.

Herman invited a woman to visit him—Karl didn't recall the year. She arrived, spent a few days with Herman, and promised to return. Several weeks later Herman contacted her, and asked when she would arrive. The woman wrote back and told him that she would never consider living so far out in the country on a filthy little dirt farm. Herman told Karl that the woman asked, "What do you think, I will cook, wash, and clean for you?" Herman responded on a postcard, "What the hell you think I want you here for; to play with your tits?"

You can't do that," Karl said, "Everyone will see it."

"Why do you think I did it that way?" Herman said.

Herman took full advantage of the postwar GI Bill. Beyond attending free classes in Bemidji, he purchased new equipment from retooled factories that had been manufacturing tanks and trucks three years earlier. With his GI Bill loan guarantee, he purchased an Allis Chalmers fertilizer spreader, a John Deere sickle mower, an Allis Chalmers side delivery rake, and a Farmall H tractor to pull the implements.

During WWII, the U.S. made huge technological leaps. After the war many of those gains converted to improved productivity in the private sector. Agriculture made great strides. Equipment got bigger and more efficient. New chemicals had been discovered; fertilizers, pesticides, and herbicides created a boom in the grain industry—especially corn.

Before WWII, the majority of beef was grass fed until they went to slaughter. Post war, with the glut of corn, feed lots were developed and the U.S. consumer discovered the tenderness of "grain-fed" beef. Seventy years later we are advised not to eat "grain-fed" beef because of the high cholesterol content. Grass-fed beef has made a comeback.

DDT, a WWII miracle pesticide developed to fight malaria, typhus, and other insect borne diseases, saved countless lives during the war and converted readily to agricultural use afterward. I imagine Herman learned about its applications and began using it to kill flies in the barn. I remember as a child spraying our stanchioned milk cows until the pesticide dripped off their flanks, the mist settling into the raw milk. DDT was banned in 1972 because it was toxic to wildlife and humans.

1948

Apparently Herman utilized his "Special $5.00 Service" but I didn't find any letters women wrote to him. It's curious to note that Herman first ordered this Certificate of Service in February, 1947. There are five rubber stamps on the back side. (Two illegible in text). Did Herman contact five women, the stamps authorizing, verifying his membership?

JAN - 4 1948

FORM OF FIRST LETTER

DATE----JAN-6---1948-----------

Dear Madam:-

By virtue of the introduction granted through the Standard Correspondence Club, Grayslake, Ill., and under the recommendation of Ella Schlosser Davis, I am taking the liberty of addressing you. She has given me a few facts regarding yourself, but I would be pleased to have you give me a more detailed description of yourself and your surroundings. I will give herewith a description of myself, and if there are any questions you may wish to ask, I will be glad to answer them. If interested and you have not already selected a suitable correspondent I shall be more than pleased to hear from you in return, and I promise that in the future, letters from me will prove more entertaining.

Very respectfully,

(P. S.)—Enclosed find stamp for reply.

MAR 4 1948

NOTICE!—A word about the "Special $5.00 Service."

At any time should you desire to take advantage of this proposition you can return this certificate with $ more and it will be accepted as $5.00 cash.

I will send your description to about Two Thousand ladies who want gentleman correspondents. This Plan seldom fails to bring the desired results and offine a speedy marriage.

Somewhere there is an Ideal Wife waiting for you. Try this Plan and see if your luck don't change. State if you want the letters to come direct to you or in my care.

Ella Schlosser Davis,
Grayslake, Ill.

(Back side of "Certificate of Service")

As I mentioned earlier, I used Herman's VA records to explore his history. What prompted him to visit a VA hospital in 1948? That medical report states,

This is a red-faced, sthenic (strong), thick-chested 41 year old man with a fringe of brown hair and bald vertex. Skin is clear. Blood pressure 130/92 on repeated measurements. Pulse 70 and regular. Respiration 18. Eyes are blue. Pupils are equal, regular and react to light normal. EOM and conjunctivae normal. Nose and ears normal. Upper partial dental plate. Teeth are dirty and worn down. Chews snuice [tobacco]. Tonsils small and pharynx reddened. Thyroid and lymph nodes not enlarged. Chest expansion good. Lungs normal and heart tones clean and well transmitted. Abdomen of sthenic type and no scars and no palpable viscera nor masses. There is an open inguinal ring on the left but no hernia detected. Extremities are normal. No varicose veins. Feet normal. Deep reflexes normal and active. No piles. Prostate gland is smooth and full size. Genitalia are normal male.

When we were kids Herman told us how a doctor stuck a finger up his butt (prostate exam). I believe that Herman was so embarrassed by the 1948 genital and prostate exam that he never returned to the VA Hospital. To my knowledge, after that appointment he rarely visited a doctor until he lay on his deathbed twenty-two years later, when he died of kidney failure due to prostate complications. I remember in late 1968 when I came home on convalescent leave, I rode into Bemidji with him. He had to stop to urinate two times within the twenty-mile drive. Two years later he died.

1949

Herman accelerated his search in 1949. He received the latest edition of *Standard Correspondence Club* and subscribed to a new singles newspaper, *Cupid's Columns,* *"Foremost Matrimonial Magazine in the World."*

He discovered my mother. She must have purchased a long-term advertisement in *Cupid's Columns* that began running the spring of 1949 because my grandmother, in her diary on August 11, 1949, wrote my mother's address, 1871 Walton Avenue. That address is listed in the key for the January-February 1950 issue of *Cupid's Columns.* (Note my mother's alias.)

472—Linda Curry, 1871 Walton Ave., Bronx 53, N. Y.

She wrote, *Charming, attractive, pretty, refined brunette. 28, 5 ft. 41/2 in., 129 lbs. College educated. Plays piano and sings. I am wonderful cook and housekeeper. Know how to farm or ranch. Would love to correspond with farmer or rancher, or any respectable gentleman who loves children. I have 4 children, 7, 5, 3, 1. Would like to meet someone who would sincerely love my children and make them his own and be a good father to them, since they lost their own. My children would be a great help to a farmer or rancher in later years, however any gentleman who thinks he could love my children will be considered. Am willing to go any place in the world for the right man.*

Did Herman subscribe to *Cupid's Columns*, a Minnesota based publication, hoping to find a local woman after so many years of searching? We'll never really know. He must have discovered my mother in an earlier edition of *Cupid's Columns* because this surviving copy, dated January-February 1950, was delivered to the farm several months after we arrived.

Other women listed financial assets as a modern-day dowry; my mother listed four children. It's the only advertisement, of hundreds of women, which mention young children. I imagine having children was a detriment to finding a man, so those men who were unsuccessful connecting with a single woman might resort to a woman with children.

There is no surviving correspondence between my mother and Herman so I try to imagine what they may have written to each other. From the information in her advertisement, we know what she promised Herman. What might he have replied? The following is my version of what Herman may have written to my mother.

Dear Linda,

Thank you for your last letter. You ask if I can imagine the crowds of New York City. Yes, I can imagine. I shipped out of Norfolk, Virginia, in 1942. We got a weekend pass and me and some buddies went downtown. I never saw so many people, and one of the guys—he was from Chicago—kept laughing at me because I kept looking up at the tall buildings. You mention not wanting to raise your kids in the city; well here on the farm they can have a good life. I grew up here and my fondest memories are playing in the woods and fishing in the near-by lake. It's a long ride from New York to Bemidji but I truly think you will love it here with the kids. I can teach them how to hunt and fish and farm. With their help and yours we can have a good life. I plan to build a new barn and triple the size of my dairy herd. I bought a purebred Holstein bull and next spring will be the first crop of calves from him. I hope to get heifer calves to build the herd. Once the barn is built, we can put in an indoor bathroom and hot water. Please say yes to visiting me.

Your friend, (I hope), Herman

One area of Herman's agricultural classes probably focused on genetics and the importance of a high quality breeding bull, which every farmer and rancher knows constitutes fifty percent of the herd's performance. On July 29, 1949, Herman purchased Prince Cornucopia Veeman, son of King Gypsie and Snowflake De Kol Veeman. His seven cows were now serviced by a prince, and would be for the next several years.

I remember that bull. Herman put a ring in his nose, connected to a ten inch chain. The theory was, when the bull dropped his head and charged, he would step on the chain. I don't think he ever actually charged anyone. I think he was just very tame. We didn't have a fence around the house so the cows could walk right up to the door. I recall my mother out in the yard, whacking the bull on the head with a broom, trying to drive him away.

Herman made other improvements, too. In the far north, hay harvest is of paramount importance for winter survival of livestock. Jayhawk hay stackers were originally powered by two horses—one on each side. By 1949, Herman had retrofitted the twelve-foot-wide contraption to the front of his new Farmall tractor. The stacker had eight-foot-long hardwood tines—probably ash. The operator drove down the windrow of dried hay, slowly weaving from side to side so the hay was evenly distributed on the tines; once full, the load was raised hydraulically and driven to an area near the barn where it was dumped onto a growing haystack.

I imagine that just as Herman mentally reviewed women in the catalogues while he was shoveling snow in the dead of winter, he did the same while working his fields in summer heat. By the summer of 1949, he was focused on my mother.

After searching for so many years, he must have been pensive the morning of our arrival. From the VA report we know he got up early to do chores. He was a very private man, never sharing his thoughts, so we can never really know his secret feelings. I remember him, when he wasn't angry, as a caring man who sometimes played little jokes, like taking his false teeth out and snapping them between his fingers at us.

I paint this possible scenario of that last night he spent alone on the farm before my mother arrived with my three siblings and me.

Sitting against the stump, Herman looked across Maple Lake through the drizzling dawn at the cedar tree line on the east side. He pulled the mildew-smelling horse hide robe close against the chill as Shep pushed her nose under his hand, begging for another caress. It was late autumn—unusually wet. The grass was still growing so the cows were grazing the night pasture.

The moon had been out a few hours earlier when he came out to the lake. Now he was stealing a few extra moments before driving the cows in for morning milking. The Holsteins nuzzled around him, curious at this break in routine. It was his fourth autumn home from the war.

Tonight, Linda and her four children arrive, he thought. I hope there's enough food stored away to last through the winter. She said in her letter that the kids don't eat much. I hope I'm not too backwards for her. But she said she loves living on a farm. How would she know that if she's from New York City? That photo she sent of her and the kids—it looks like a magazine picture. Little Tim is four years old—same as Bruno when he was killed. God, it's been thirty-four years since ma carried him up the driveway; her crying, her head bloody, Bruno not moving. They never did catch the bastards who honked their car and spooked the horse. Poor little Bruno.

Last night had been another sleepless night. Yesterday, he'd spent the day carrying potatoes down to the basement. Carrots and rutabagas and onions were already done—canning was finished—he was proud of his ability to cook and can. But after evening milking and supper he'd been restless—he'd washed the milk separator slowly, counting the thin steel disks unconsciously, willing himself to be tired—but he knew....

Harvest moon lighted the bedroom and he tossed for three hours trying to sleep, finally giving it up. He got up, splashed still-warm water from the cook stove reservoir over his head, and toweled it dry. With Shep at his heel he left the house, horse-hide robe tucked under his arm. The chill night breeze reminded him of the cold desert and the constant sand in Africa.

Tonight there were only soggy leaves still clinging to the plum trees in the orchard and the smell of damp dead grass as he followed his shadow toward the lake. The lake—what he and his buddies would have given for a gallon of that water back in North Africa. There was never enough to drink or wash. The sergeants' refrain about not wasting water echoed in his memory—"half a canteen to bathe and shave—drink the other half." On the bluff overlooking the lake he could hear mallards feeding in the reeds near the shore. Wrapped in the bristly old robe, he sat down, back against a stump, and stared at the moon's reflection—re-membering—finally dozing. Reflexively, he flattened to the ground at the low overhead whistle of incoming.

Awake, he realized it was not German 105mm artillery, but a flock of teals coming in to land. He watched the ducks settle, feet out, brea-

king the surface-glaze as they landed, the ducks unaware of the man ne-stled against the stump. Shep yapped at them. He stroked her head and looked down. "You're the only one that'll put up with me, ain't you." Shep leaned up and licked his face. "Come on, you mutt—let's get these cows milked."

Late that evening he paced the sidewalk outside the Greyhound sta-tion in Bemidji. He watched diesel exhaust gush from the bus as it came around the corner. Yellow light from the street lamps bathed the bus as it coasted to the curb. The door opened and four Indians filed down the steps. Then a curly dark haired boy carrying a chubby toddler with blond curls, followed by another smaller boy. A lady carrying a baby stepped down, assisted by the driver. She doesn't look like the women around here, he thought. But it must be her—she is pretty. But she wears so much lipstick. And the powder on her cheeks. Those big combs in her hair—I wonder how much those cost. And that fur wrapped around her neck—I've only seen pictures of women wearing them. He stood under the streetlamp looking at her. She glanced at him, then toward the ligh-ted stationhouse.

I don't remember the trip to Minnesota. I would love to know my mother's first impression of Herman when we stepped off the bus. Was he dressed in his suit and wearing the fedora he wore in his photo? Or was he clad in sagging dungarees, a faded blue work shirt, and wilt-brimmed hat?

Chris remembers that the bus arrived late in the evening. If that's true, Herman probably drove in after milking and smelled of the barn. Like the old farmers before him, he wore long johns all summer and rarely took a bath. He'd wash up and shave each day, but wore the same work clothes and underwear for weeks at a time. Chris said we drove out to the farm in a Plymouth Coupe. Our mother sat in the front holding

Laurel while Herman drove, with me wedged between. Chris and Tim crouched in the back.

Chris also recalls that during the first few months, as winter set in, we all slept downstairs; Herman in the bedroom, our mother and Laurel on a bed set up in the living room, and we three boys on cots near the stove in the open dining/kitchen area. Herman must have been ecstatic that autumn we arrived in Bemidji. His dream was beginning to take shape.

1950

The winter of 1949 and spring 1950 must have been a happy time. Winter 1949, Barbara holding Laurel, Chris on left, Wendell on right.

Herman was very proud of his new Farmall H tractor. In the first heady days on the farm, Barb allowed Herman to hold Laurel.

Winter 1949, on the farm in Nebish. Herman holding Laurel, Wendell on right, Chris and Tim on left.

On January 17, 1950, Barbara and Herman were married. I was two; my oldest brother, Chris, seven, remembers that neighbors came in horse-drawn sleighs for the shiveree. Barbara used the alias Linda for the first few years she lived in Minnesota—including on the marriage license. Herman had innocently fallen into this relationship—perhaps innocently is not the right word because he had been searching for four years. I wonder how long he whispered sweet nothings to "Linda" before he learned her real name.

Three months after Herman and Barbara were married, my grandmother drafted the following letter to New York Governor Dewey. Note the rusted paperclip stains from lying in the chickenhouse for almost three decades.

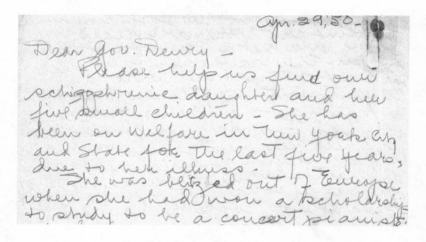

Here is the full text of the letter verbatim as written by Barb's mother.

April 29, '50

Dear Gov. Dewey –

Please help us find our schizophrenic daughter and her 5 small children. She has been on welfare in New York City and State for the last 5 years, due to her illness. She was blitzed out of Europe when she had won a scholarship to study to be a concert pianist. She had won 6 points towards the "Prix to Rome" at the Royal Conservatoire in Brussels and the French literature prize in a French school (Mlle. de Decker) that didn't take foreigners.

Since her illness she has taken to disappearing. This is very dangerous for the children, because she needs constant help. The welfare of the State has done a wonderful job. When she disappeared at Bayshore on Long Island Mrs. Mae Sloan, director, left no stone unturned until she found her. At Cooperstown Mrs. Miller was equally vigilant and had her in the care of a psychiatrically trained nurse while she was a waiting her 4th child.

But here in New York City under the Democrats they are really awful. I have never met a Protestant caseworker. They visited her only once in 6 months. They were in cahoots with Mr. Rosen, who owns the building, to get her out because she had too many children. They withheld her rent there for having her constantly plagued by sheriffs and lastly her utility money so that she was in constant fear of not being able to cook or have lights. No wonder she disappeared this time.

I have written four letters to Commissioner Hilliard and always I get referred back to the caseworker who refuses to do anything because she blames the directive that they are simply too close the case, on a directive that comes down from the State. They know we are Republicans so there are no more votes to be gotten there.

My husband is a veteran of both world wars. 5 years this last one. His business is no good since he came back wounded because the Democrats ruined it. I am Republican Capt. of my district and four-time ardent campaigner for you. I am a Vassar graduate in the days before Eleanor Roosevelt ruined our college and made it pinkish Red.

I am almost the only ardent worker in this whole Assembly District. There are about 4 others but there ought to be about 200 at least. The leaders have been in too long. They ride along on a minimum of work because they have petty jobs from the State. That's why you've lost two campaigns. The districts have never been worked house to house at all. Also we can't any longer afford to be "me–tooers."

Please read this letter and tell me what to do. If the welfare assumes the responsibility of her support they must also assume the responsibility of her well-being. Dr. Phyllis Greenacre also Dr. Cole, also Dr. Berkeley of New York Hospital considers her the "fluttery type," and recommends a sanatorium at $75 a week for her cure.

We are penniless because we have spent all we have on her. No such treatment is possible, but with the help of the Welfare we could see that the children are not in grave danger – such as many a child of a mentally ill person. They are wonderful children and worthy of saving – so is she.

Because of my political work in the District please don't let this get in the papers and please advise me as to how I can get the welfare and Missing Persons Bureau to looking for our daughter, as she is on welfare somewhere in a big city where they do not pay any attention to them. As you well know, this type of illness, they sneak into a shadow somewhere, which is so bad for those warm hearted little boys.

Sincerely E. F. P.[Elsie Fratt Philips]

So this is a glimpse of the woman Herman married, the woman who used the name Linda on their marriage license. The woman who was hiding from her parents because she feared they would commit her to a mental institution and take custody of us children. I think my mother had a legitimate fear, because my grandmother wrote, "… with the help of the Welfare we could see that the children are not in grave danger…." It sounds as though she did want custody and expected the Welfare Department to pay her. Historical note: There were only four children when my grandmother drafted this letter, but that's another story.

Herman's first son, Randy, was born January 30, 1951. The spring of 1952 my mother loaded us onto a Greyhound bus and we left Herman. We first spent a few weeks living in Elko, Nevada, and then moved to a small cabin on a mountainside near Stehekin, Washington. Late that autumn, destitute and hungry, we returned to Herman. Three more children were born over the next several years; Bonnie in 1954, Linda in 1955, Larry in 1957.

After a decade of acrimony and spousal abuse, nine months pregnant with her ninth child, my mother made her last escape attempt in December of 1960. Herman wrote the following letter to my grandmother. Again, like so many of the thousands of letters I rescued, note the mold stains from decades in the chickenhouse.

Here is the full text of the letter verbatim as written by Herman.

Puposky, Minn.

Jan 4, 1960

Dear Mother—

The Rev. Daniels was just hear and his report is bad very bad matter of fact its so bad that I'm afraid for the kids sake what will happen to them and I'm at a loss as to what to do. First, Chris and Tim are out of hand Barb cannot handle them. The Minister seemed to think they would take off, steal a car and land in jail. Barb still insists she is going to Seattle and if they forced her to come back she would put in for a divorce. The Rev told her she would not gain anything by that. The welfare would step in and take all the kids and put them in homes one here and another there and she give him a big horse laugh. He said he could not handle her and wondered how I did and I told him I have not always been to fortunate either that if she got a brainstorm in her head all hell and damnation could not stop her. He said, I see what you [sic]. He said she had another boy and a big one weight 10lb10oz and she did almost die. No wonder the hospital sent word to get me at her bedside but the welfare did not tell me that. Oh Boy, Oh Boy, what a headache no wonder men get gray, bald, and die ahead of time, these women. If this one quits me there will never be another. One is enough for me and if I lose my family I'll sell everything I got as there will be nothing to look forward to, nothing to work for. In plain English (I'll just give up, quit.) Your true son (we hope) Herman P.S. Will keep you posted.

I mentioned earlier that we could never know Herman's secret thoughts because he was so private. This letter reveals the angst he felt at the loss of his family.

I was two the autumn we moved to Minnesota so Herman was the only father I ever knew. Many times as I unraveled my parents' past, I've wondered if he had found a local girl who hadn't seen the world, or a girl who had grown up during the Depression on a subsistence farm, a girl who would have worked beside him, would they have made a successful life together? I like to think so.

PART II

Attic Treasures

After my mother died in 2010 I discovered thousands of documents, dating from 1822-1984, locked in the chickenhouse on our old farm homestead in northern Minnesota. The collection comprised a history of my maternal ancestors and a very detailed, intimate record of my mother's life.

I spent countless hours sorting, analyzing, and scanning letters, diary pages, photographs, and legal documents. As I studied Barb's past, I came to realize that she did the best she was capable of doing. In the end, on her deathbed, she changed her will, and gave me ownership of the treasure trove she was leaving behind: our family's collective past that some of my siblings wanted to burn.

The many twists and turns in my mother's life challenged me to find the truest door into her story. Beyond the treasures in the chickenhouse, I discovered several 1940s lonely hearts club catalogues upstairs in the old farmhouse. They were singles publications Herman had ordered after he returned to the farm from World War II.

In the dead of winter, I sat on the rough-cut board floor in the unheated attic, bundled in wool coveralls and a parka as I thumbed through the fragile pages with frosty fingers. I discovered my mother's picture and advertisement in *Cupid's Columns,* and it seemed the natural starting point to explore my parents' lives.

I think each generation carries a unique burden. Today, as a grandparent, I worry about the world we are leaving our children: a world rife with debt, with cyber security issues and global terrorism; a world of social media, electronic communications, and medical breakthroughs unimagined a few decades ago.

My parents' generation came of age during the Great Depression of the 1930s and World War Two (WWII) from 1941-1945. Millions of men marched off to war. Millions of women stepped forward, into uncharted territory, as they left the role of homemaker and farmer's daughter to power the machines that made President Franklin Delano Roosevelt's (FDR) "Arsenal of Democracy" a reality.

The bombing of Pearl Harbor by the Japanese on December 7, 1941, triggered not only the United States' entry into WWII; it also accelerated the modern women's movement, as women entered the wartime workforce. In the post war years, many of those women refused to return meekly to the function of homemaker. This was the bridal pool Herman was searching.

In the following pages, I offer a brief glimpse of the role of women in society during that era.

Perhaps the most captivating account I discovered about those turbulent years was *Our Mothers' War* by Emily Yellin, documenting the contributions and wartime experiences of her mother, Carol Lynn Gilmer. One of the things that drew me to Yellin's book was that she, like me, had discovered her mother's old letters in her attic after her mother died. I understood the excitement she wrote about in the Prologue, upon discovering those old accounts.

Suddenly, sitting on the attic floor, I was beginning to realize there were more dimensions in my mother's wartime experience than I knew. I saw then it had been a transforming time for her, a time when she first came into her own, exerted her courage and took advantage of new opportunities for herself, as a woman. In those letters and pictures, and her

diary, I began to see the war through a new lens, a female perspective.
It was an unfamiliar but intriguing view.

Our Mother's War documents the activities, challenges, struggles, and triumphs, of millions of women during the war years. As I read about Carol Lynn Gilmer, I found myself empathizing with my mother, as she navigated those turbulent years, divorced, with young children. Unlike the author's mother, who "…came into her own," my future mother found herself in uncharted waters, bouncing from shoal to shoal.

I discovered a second treasure as I read *Our Mother's War*: Yellin's extensive endnotes—the link to better understanding dynamics that both of our mothers and their generation of women faced in the 1940s. Reading about the millions of girls and women who left farms and families and moved to cities for wartime work, I thought again of the hundreds of advertisements in the singles publications I had inherited and wondered how many of those women returned to farm and family after the war but chafed at the limited prospects they faced.

They had been exposed to a larger world, a world beyond the confines of rural isolation. After several years of city living, working next to strange men on assembly lines, those young women were no longer intimidated by the unknown and had the courage to reach out in a post war society that was in complete flux: they reached out through lonely hearts club advertisements.

A significant layer of this *1940s Lonely Hearts Search* is the historical insights these singles catalogues offer. They shed a glimmer of light on the plight of single women, a segment of society without the social or financial safety nets we have today. These women were forced to take risks—some became isolated on small dirt farms, where they were destined to spend their lives.

The lonely hearts club catalogues I discovered in the attic were pre-integration: "This Club is for the White Race only" proclaims *Standard Correspondence Club*. The term "catalogue" was often used to describe organized client lists in singles publications. As I thumbed through the eggshell pages, I felt compelled to learn more and began an Internet search.

Unlike the 1940s singles publications that placed an emphasis on the woman's education, religion, and net worth, at first glance, many of today's dating sites promote sexuality. I didn't find any 1940s singles catalogues on the internet but I learned that newspaper "Personals" had evolved, using the same language of single-letter abbreviations to create a universally recognized three letter acronym. For example, DLF means divorced Latina female—there's a whole vocabulary of acronyms, including sexual orientation.

When I Googled dating club history, "Hot online dating" popped up. College coeds to senior citizens wooed me. The search list went on: "Married dating club" (Why be married, I wondered), "Cougar dating club," "Gay dating club," "Kenyan dating club." You get the picture—someone for everyone. "Our trusted dating site matches couples on 29 dimensions of compatibility for long lasting relationships," promised eHarmony.com.

I learned that today's dating options have expanded along with resources to order background checks. Many dating sites scan potential clients for a history of sexual assault, identity theft, violence, and marital status.

Few people today remember Raymond Fernandez and Martha Beck, serial killers who lured up to twenty women, many in New York City, to their deaths through lonely hearts club ads between 1947 and 1949—the exact years my mother advertised herself, my three siblings, and me. Fernandez and Beck were eventually found guilty and executed by electric chair at Sing Sing Prison on March 8, 1951. I wonder if they read my mother's ad but were dissuaded because of us children.

There were no compatibility filters or criminal background check options to screen possible suitors, so it's not hard to imagine the frightful situations some women were duped into. Reading the yellowed advertisements I had discovered in the attic, I was struck by how much society has changed over the past seventy years.

At the time Pearl Harbor was bombed in 1941, there were twelve million women—females fourteen years and older—in the workforce. By 1944 that number had jumped to sixteen and a half million— a 36 percent increase. (One source reports nineteen million.) The number of women in management and official positions jumped more than 50 percent. Nonfarm craftsmen, foremen, etc., saw similar rises for women. Other occupations also saw increases: sales, 60 percent; farm workers, 19 percent; clerical, 85 percent. It's interesting to note, even during wartime, the glass ceiling held firm; professional opportunities for women increased less than two percent.

By 1946, twelve million men had returned to the civilian workforce. The Employment Act of 1946 was designed to transition the economy from a wartime footing to peacetime full employment. It appears to foreshadow modern-day bureaucracy. The main results were the creation of several government advisory committees and no tangible results for the civilian workforce.

Postwar interviews in 1946 revealed that up to ninety percent of all women who worked in wartime positions hoped and expected to keep them. Ninety-six percent of single and divorced women and 98 percent of widows planned to continue in their wartime industrial positions.

Today, most married women retain an individual identity, but in the 1940s, it was the social norm for a woman to introduce herself as an extension of her husband. For example, my great grandmother, in a letter to my grandmother in 1943, signed herself Mrs. C.D. [Charles Diller] Fratt; the addressee, my grandmother, was identified as Mrs. Henry Philips.

After the men returned from WWII and reclaimed their jobs, millions of women lost their new-found independence and were relegated back to the role of housewife. Divorce rates skyrocketed and singles catalogues flourished as men and women searched for that new perfect life-mate. As I researched the 1940s catalogues, I came to realize that, like many events from our past, the predicament of single women in post WWII society had been marginalized.

It's difficult today to visualize the information isolation of the 1940s, especially in areas where rural electrification had not reached. Many small farms did not even have a direct current battery-powered radio, so newspapers and magazines were their window to the world. There is a psychological layer to the lonely hearts catalogues, how they marketed to the insecurities of their audience. Fear was a marketing tool. In 1945, Ella Schlosser Davis, Editor of *Standard Correspondence Club*, wrote in her introductory column: ...*you do not know what it means to live alone, uncared for, unknown, when old age overtakes you; solitude fills one with horrible agony. Solitude at home by the fireside at night is so profound, so sad.*

The U.S. lost more than 400,000 men during the war. Many women advertised themselves as, "widow by death," others as, "widow by divorce." In combing through the singles catalogues, I was surprised at how many women over fifty were looking for a new man. I imagine many felt lost, confused, financially vulnerable, even though they listed assets—a sort of modern day dowry.

While I worked on a memoir about life on our farm in the 1950s, my stepfather and mother's plight kept pulling me back to the brittle catalogues. Each one of the thousands of women who advertised in lonely hearts listings had a story—a story I hope was more gratifying than my mother's.

DECEMBER 11, 1945

THE EXCHANGE CLUB

Some singles publications had a list of names tucked with them—others did not. The name list will precede the publication the women are listed in. Notes written in page margins were done by my stepfather, Herman, as he searched for a wife during the 1940s.

1-Myrtis M. Wolfer, P.O. Box 127,
Honey Island, Texas.
2-Maude Yattaw, RR 1,. Manchester, Tenn.
3-Gertrude Brewer Groff, 400 Astor & Airy
Sts., Norristown, Pa.
4-Canceled.
5-Mrs. Jennie Williams, RR 2, Box 712,
Texarkana, Texas.
6-Mrs. Eula G. Haulsee, 1756 - 52nd St.,
Birmingham, Ala.
7-Mrs. Lillian Rowe, 409 North St.,
Sharon Spring, Pa.
8-Bonnie Lawson, 209 Lenoir Ave. Wayne, Pa.
9-Clara Hedges, Box 33, Cazenovia, Ill.
10-Mrs. B. A. Jones, RR 5, Box 243,
Clinton, N. C.
11-Florence Schalker, P. O. Box 962,
Lansing 4, Mich.
12-Mrs. Pearl Robinson, Box 13,
Crosbyton, Texas.
13-Miss Willie Golden, RR 1,
Eagle Rock, Va.
14-Nellie M. Van Ostrand, 723 Division
Ave., York, Nebr.
15-Raymah Farr, 107 S. Bleekley Drive,
Wichita, Kans.
16-Cora Horst, 1119 Taylor, Topeka, Kans.
17-Carrie Schroeder, 139 E. Hannum St.,
Carterville, Mo.
18-Ida Burnott, 122 E. Wilson,
Carterville, Mo.
19-Mrs. Cora Lee Gates, 2208 N. Main Ave.,
Springfield, Mo.
20-Mrs. Christine M. Melton, 500 Maple
St., Daytona Beach, Fla.
21-Floy Horton, 622 Victory St.,
Little Rock, Ark.
22-Canceled.
23-Mrs. Alice Caine, 2230 Fairview,
Detroit 14, Mish.
24-Ethel M. Ogden, 922 - 17th St.,
Douglas, Ariz.
25-Miss Luella Braden, RR 1, Box 194,
Bragg City, Mo.
26-Canceled.
27-Miss Ruby B. Embry, 203 Hinkle St.,
Townsville, N. C.

28-Mrs. A. C. Burch, RR 2,Gardners, Pa.
29-Georgia E. Morrell,Millers Ferry, Fla.
30-Julia Sellers, 307 Monroe, Washington,
Ill.
31-Canceled.
32-Mrs. Alma Callahan, Turkey, Ky.
33-Susan Meredith, 1620 Ohio Ave.,
Lansing-6, Mich.
34 Canceled.
35-Ida Cotter, 521 - 11th St.,
Clarkston, Wash.
36-Lillian Bostrom, 1626 S.E. Alder,
Apt. 7, Portland 14, Oregon.
37-Lillian Olsten,6624 Miramonte Blvd.,
Los Angeles, Calif.
38-Mrs. Josie Sheffield, Box 1440,
Mount Ida, Ark.
39-Julia Pressley, 2123 N. Brandywine,
Arlington, Va.
40-Mrs. Verna D. Randolph, 53 N.Somerville,
Memphis, Tenn.
41-Alice M. Smith,Box 733,Canton.#### Ohio.
42-Opal Wiggins, G.D. Talequah, Okla.
43-Grace Cline, 2308 Douglas St.,
Omaha, Nebr.
44-Mrs. Dixie Seamonds, 57 Water St.,
Logan, #### W. Va.
45-Marie E. La Couture, 205 Willow St.,
Woonsocket, R. I.
46-Maudie Foreman, 623 Rogers,
Springfield, Mo.
47-Mrs. Della Stullings, Newton, N. C.
48-Mrs. Mary Romsing, 96 Burnet St.,
New. Brunswick, N. J.
Mary Baker, 512 Tenn. Ave., N. E.
Washington, D. C.
50-Mrs.Effie Pritchett, 2959 Avenue 'Z'
Fairview, Birmingham, Ala.
51-Mrs. Clara Templeton, 119 Edison St.,
McMinnville, Tenn.
52-Jennie Murdock, 88 N, West St.,
Hillsdale, Mich.
53-Mrs. Agnes D. Broadway, Hospital,
Roanoke Rapids, N. C.
54-Mrs. Hattie M. Workman, 506 'C' St.,
La Porte, Ind.
55-Netta Mencer, Oldtown, Maryland.

56-Mrs. Delia Aysien, 2001 Prytania St.,
New Orleans, La.
57-Florence Heward, 2145 brighton St.,
Burbank, Calif.
58-Canceled.
59-Bertha B. Covert, RR 6,Lakeview,
Oregon.
60-Mrs. Syble Massey, Box 333, Naples, Ten
61-Annie E. Hughes, 608 Cleveland St.,
Charleston, Mo.
62-Miss Loraine Elliott, 415 Spring St.,
Clarksville, Tenn.
63-Evelyn Parry, 3376 W. 125th St.,
Cleveland 11, Ohio.
64-Mrs. Etta Mills, 1821 San Fernando
Road, Los Angeles 41, Calif.
65-Mrs. Cara Megaffin, Box 277, Pratt,
Kansas.
66-Mildred McCarthy, G.D. Merced, Calif.
67-Mattie Ratliff, RR 1, Colony, Okla.
68-Mrs. Loretta Staneler, 920 W. Blackwell
Ave.,Mrs.Alice Weekner, Blackwell, Okla.
69-Audria Lawson, 107 Crawford St.,
Willows, Calif.
70-Mary De Noyer, P. O. Box 57, Sta. 'F',
Toledo 10, Ohio.
71-Mrs. Mary O'Donnell, RR 1, Box 83,
Perkins, Okla.
72-Mrs. Odessa S. Ross, 615 Pleasant
Place, Akron, Ohio.
73-Mrs. Rilla Walker, P. O. Box 132,
Cherokee, Okla.
74-Virginia E. Cochran, RR 2, Box 12,
Beale, Florida.
75-Mrs. Grace Smith, 11421 Camden Ave.,
Detroit 13, Mich.
76-Canceled.
77-Mrs. Jessie Tillery, 1242#######
Edgemont, Hollywood 27, Calif.
78-Martha Clayton, RR 1, Wynne, Ark.
79-Mrs. Lula Quisinberry, 513 E. Division
St., Springfield, Mo.
80-Mrs. Mary Whitlinger, 1811 W. First
St., Duluth, Minn.
81-Althea Hughes, Louis Valley Route 1,
Marietta, Okla.
82-Mrs. Ruth Larper,RR 3, Carrollton, Mo.

83-Mrs. Bessie Lewis, 119 Mass. Ave.,
Jackson, Miss.
84-Rose B. Macy, 312 E. Vermont,
Indianapolis, Ind.
85-L. Jane Richardson, 4014 Drexel Blvd.,
Chicago 15, Ill.
86-Mrs. V. L. Tennyson, Gen. Del.,
Pensacola, Fla.
87-Mabel Crook, 206 S. 10th St.,
* Tonkawa, Okla.
88-Canceled.
89-Mrs. Meadie Parker, RR1,Tremont, Miss.
90-Bertha Oldfield, RR 1, Beach, N. Dak.
91-Myrtle Morgan, RR 1, Braggs, Okla.
92-Miriam M. Gromis, 550 N. 10th St.,
Reading, Pa.
93-Jean Levitt, 2552 Taylor, Apt. 5,
Detroit 6, Mich.
94-Grace Leicht, P.O. Box 66, Union, Mo.
95-Victoria Farkas, P. O. Box 1162,
Enid, Okla.
96-Mrs. Dora Burger, Putney, W. Va.
97-Ruth Clay, 528 E. New York St.,
Indianapolis, Ind.
98-Mrs. Nila Gray, 513 W. Cumberland Ave.,
Knoxville, Tenn.
99-Mattie Van Dusen, 710 Berger St.,
Malvern, Ark.
100-Agnes Warner, Box 1134, Salina, Kans.
101-Mrs. Rettie Allen, 507 Gardner St.,
Joliet, Ill.
102-Jessie Gatewood, Cabool, Mo.
103-Loétte C. Wise, P. O. Box 522,
Port Saint Joe, Fla.
104-Teresa Ryan, 1688 E. 46th St.,
Brooklyn 3, N. Y.
105-Mary Moosher, 610 Doughty Rd.,
Pleasantville, N. J.
106-Miss Gladys Andrews, Box 022,
New Sharon, Iowa.
107-Mrs. Ina Pierce,RR 2, Jamestown, Ky.
108-Mrs. Drue Brandon, 720 Mill St.,
Manchester, Tenn.
109-Mrs. Frankie Rhoads, 210 Main St.,
Paris, Mo.
110-Mrs. Mary Lash, 808 Maumee St.,
Adrian, Mich.

111-Pattie L. Clark, 810 Clark St.,
Greenville, N. C.
112-Miss Bertha Smith, Canaan, Vermont.
113-Miss Shirley M. Hartley, 611 North
Park, Springfield, Mo.
114-Mrs. Nellie Hall, P. O. Box 833,
Rockford, Ill.
115-Gertrude Haugbro, 16 W. Caster St.,
Dexter, Mo.
116-Mrs. Janie Dull, RR 2, Buffalo, Mo.
117-Mrs. Myrtle Brookshier, Gen. Del.,
Wichita Falls, Texas
118-Susie Babuchna, RR 2, %C. B. Baylis,
Moselle, Miss.
119-Alverta Townsend, Oliphant Furnace, Pa.
120-Mrs. Minnie Shoup, RR 2, Meadville, Pa.
121-Mrs. G. Ross, P. O. Box 328,
Sumter, S. C.
122-Mae S. Mills, 317½ N. Pen Ave.,
Independence, Kans.
123-Mrs. Nellie Snow, RR 2, Rockwood, Tenn.
124-Nora Blanton, Box 121, Paintsville, Ky.
125-Alice E. Halsey, 8 Brigham Road,
Worcester, Mass.
126-Mrs. Hazel Cessell, Navy Galley,
University of Louisville, Louisville, Ky.
127-Mrs. Ida E. Slanker, 438 N. Sarah,
Apt. 5, St. Louis 8, Mo.
128-Miss Dora L. Wooten, RR 5,
El Dorado, Ark.
129-Mrs. Lillian Welsch, 720 S. Muldrow
St., Mexico, Mo.
130-Mrs. M. B. Lockley, 847 N. 20th St.,
Philadelphia, Pa.
131-Betty Ann M. Davis, Gen. Del.,
Beverly Hills, Calif.
132-Mamie Foreman, Lamar, Mo.
133-Mrs. K. Lakens, 907 Ponce De Leon Ave.,
Atlanta, Ga.
134-Mrs. Jewell Willis, RR 1,
Stephensville, Texas.
135-Miss Ada Carter, Wharncliffe, W. Va.
136-Bernice Stephenson, P. O. Box 158,
League City, Texas.
137-Mrs. Grace Baumgardner, 213 Cherry
St. Chattanooga 3, Tenn.
138-Nancy Dyehouse, 221 W. Monroe St.,
Princeton, Ind.

139-Mrs. Bertha Casey, 423 Fairmont,
Jackson, Tenn.
140-Mrs. Bessie Reynolds, RR 6, %J. B. Bate
Yakima, Wash.
141-Mrs. Alice Gray, 1578 Union St.,
San Bernardine, Calif.
142-Miss Ada King, RR 2, Box 298,
Jasper, Ala.
143-Jewell Samms, McClure, Ill.
144-Mrs. Ada Ehrman, 310 N. Persons St.,
Raleigh, N. C.
145-Mrs. Beatrice Sullivan, RR 1,
Bradfordsville, Ky.
146-Myrtle Mrohs, 1738 Colorado Ave.,
Flint 6, Mich.
147-Mrs. Annia Baxter, Jerome, Idaho.
148-Miss Iva Williams, Hitchita, Okla.
149-Mrs. Olive B. Haney, 203 E. North St.,
Brookfield, Mo.
150-Mrs. C. Christiansen, P. O. Box 62,
Phenix City, Ala.
151-Mrs. Jennie Mae Webb, 1602 Bidwell St.
Pittsburgh 12, Pa.
152-Mary Dyke, RR 3, Box 188,
Bartlesville, Okla.
153-Mrs. Maude Riggins, 505 N. Barnes St.,
Bushnell, Ill.
154-Dorothy Oberkrom, Fulton, Mo.
155-Mrs. W. S. Smith, RR 3, Ti, Okla.
156-Mrs. C. L. A Cobbs, 610 Walnut St.,
Knoxville 30, Tenn.
157-Mary A. Aston, 3521 High St.,
%Ruth Kepner, Oakland 2, Calif.
158-Florence Wendebarn, RR 2, Lubbock,
Texas.
159-Elizabeth Wassberg, RFD, Central Islip,
N. Y.
160-Josephine Baker, 1031 N. Ogden Dr.,
Hollywood 46, Calif.
161-Blance Innis Nichols, 1404 Central
Ave., Kansas City, Kans.
162-Lillie Mae Williams, 47th St. Grocery,
West Monroe, La.
163-Kay Bruce, Box 184, Park Falls, Wis.
164-Mrs. Verna Smith, RR 1, Box 45-A,
Randleman, N. C.
165-Mrs. Ellen Mann, 1901 Bay Ave.,
Hampton, Va.

166-Miss Patricia Yost, RR 1, Box 2,
Grand Rapids, Mich.
167-Frances M. Bloch, 8920 - 161st St.,
Jamaica, N. Y.
168-Emma A. Evitt, 3218 W. Monroe St.,
Chicago, Ill.
169-Miraim McMullin, Box 772, Great Bend,
Kans.
170-Georgia Osborne, Box 62, Brownville,
Nebr.
171-Alice Loona Nelson, Box 108,
Polk, Nebr.
172-Docia Beidelman, 333 W. Chase St.,
Springfield, Mo.
173-Mary A. Haelin, RR 2, Can Run Road,
Shively, Ky.
174-Dolores Cotton, RR 3, Box 21,
North Little Rock, Ark.
175-Hettie Bartlett, 259 Orchard Ave.,
Cuyahoga Falls, Ohio.
176-Mrs. Lilly McRae, 1925 W. 12th Ave.,
Pine Bluff, Ark.
177-Luella Rehmert, 2426 Wayne Ave.,
Dayton, Ohio.
178-Miss Maude Burton, 17 Johnson St.,
Reidsville, N. C.
179-Bernice Delcamp, 215 S. Homer,
Lansing, Mich.
180-Eunice Kelley, 21 Fisher St.,
Fort Fairfield, Maine.
181-Mrs. Stella Barrick, 532 - 2nd St.,
Lincoln, Ill.
182-Mrs. Lewey Fuller, Drill, Va.
183-Mario Hathaway, 750 S. State St.,
Elgin, Ill.
184-Moulie Hall, Pines Rd. RR 1,
Paterson, N. J.
185-Elsie 146-10 Linden Blvd.,
Jamaica 4, N. Y.
186-Sadie M. Smith, 101 E. Montgomery
Ave., N.S. Pittsburgh 12, Pa.
187-Stella Little, 724 E. Grand St.,
Springfield, Mo.
188-Mary Ann Adams, Box 7, Hemet, Calif.
189-Edna S. Bach, Box 272, Jackson, Ky.
190-Mrs. Grace Coston, RR 4, Box 23-A,
Orlando, Fla.
191-Minnie Seaman, 124 N. Tucker St.,
Shawnee, Okla.

192—Miss Di Ann Beard, 55 Hibiscus
Island, Miami Beach, Fla.
193—Ada Wrey, North Salem, Ind.
194—Clara E. Haskett, 216 N. Maple,
Commerce, Okla.
195—Mrs. Cecil Seibert, 1108 Oak St.,
Frankfort, Ind.
196—Lottie Fulkerson, RR 1, Stella, Mo.
197—Mrs. Maude Brainow, 1417 W. 3rd St.,
Little Rock, Ark.
198—Nancee Stump, 1507 N. 5th St.,
Quincy, Ill.
199—Cora Givens, 718 N. Commerce,
Gainesville, Texas
200—Ella Furr, Box 135, Midland, N. C.
201—May Benner, 119 Court St.,
Burlington, Iowa.
202—Ora B. Wilson, 227 N. Church
St., Hudson, Mich.
203—Birdie L. Hoisington, RR 5,
Shawnee, Okla.
204—Faye Mitchell, Civilian Dormitory
#465, Fort Leonard Wood, Mo.
205—Della B. Long, 1445 W. State St.,
Rockford, Ill.
Erma Krein, 4168 Duquesne Ave.,
Culver City, Calif.
207—Clara Snyder, 320 Pleasant St.,
Ithaca, N. Y.
208—Mrs. C. V. Rhodes, RR 2, Freedom, Me.
209—Mrs. Annie A. Edwards, 1113 W. Cave
Springs, El Dorado, Kans.
210—Miss Cora Smith, RR 3, Crab Orchard,
Ky.
211—Miss Rose Gallien, 549½ Jordan St.,
Shreveport, La.
212—Helen Daywood, 2703 E. 1st St.,
Austin 22, Texas.
213—Mrs. Bonnie Hastings, 100 S. Paris,
Antlers, Okla.
214—Mrs. Josie Martin, Box 33, Waltham,
Maine.
215—Miss Evelyn I. Moose, 610 W. 7th St.,
Newton, N. C.
216—Mrs. May Piatt, Chester, W. Va.
217—Mrs. Marie Schroeder, 1506 E. 24th
St., Minneapolis, Minn.
218—Mrs. Sadie C. Wilson, 850 Alice St.,
Waycross, Ga.

219-Mrs. R. A. Melton, RR 1, Box 140,
Mount Croghan, S. C.
220-Josephine Oliver, Pinecrest Sani-
torium, Beckley, W. Va.
221-Mrs. Ella Lee, 802 N. 4th St.,
Garden City, Kans.
222-Mrs. Jimmie Lou Shelton, RR 1, Box
42, Holcomb, Miss.
223-Mrs. Fatherine Miller, 56 Jackson St.,
Coldwater, Mich.
224-Maude Farley, 600 Lincoln Ave.,
Monett, Mo.
Mrs. Ross Clark, RR 1, Milo, Mo.
226-Martha V. King, 2053 Liberty Blvd.,
South Gate, Calif.
227-Hattie C. Mattox, 712 S. Lake,
Okmulgee, Okla.
228-Mrs. Virginia Beggs, RR 2,Altha, Fla.
229-Alice Schoonbormer,Bloomfield. Nebr.
230-Mollie C. Kidwell, Box 150,
Mendon, Mich.
231-Mrs. Lena Scott, Box 40, Iaeger,W. Va,
232-Canceled.
233-Mrs. Marie Burke, Box 5, Vidette, Ga.
234-Sarah B. Bernard, Phil, Ky.
235-Julia Lockmon, Star Rte.Squires, Mo.
236-Maude McGarvey, 507 Porter,Alton, Ill.
237-Susan L. Casteel, Box 583, Cheyenne
Wyo.
238-Malena Fuqua, 430 S. 1st St.,
Warrington, Fla.
239-Dana E. Sawyer, RR 2, Erie, Ill.
240-Mrs. Alice Jones, 932 N. 52nd Way,
Birmingham, Ala.
241-Jessie Rowe,#319 S. Faris Ave.,
Evansville, Ind.
242-Mrs. Cora Upgraff, 401 N. Sheardian
Road, Peoria, Ill.
243-Mrs. Ethel Hutchinson, 701 Marshall-
dell, Dallas, Texas.
244-Mrs. Ella Hudnall, 128 Westwood Drive,
Beckley, W. Va.
245-Iva Mincey, 902 Maplewood,
Ypsilanti, Mich.
246-Mrs. Mary O. Kerfoot,Greenbriar, Mo.
247-Mollie Ball, Box 41, Tad, W. Va.
248-Mrs. Dora Hawley, Box 134,.
Coeur D'Alene, Idaho.

249-Mrs. Lena Manwarren, 103 N. Texas,
Cherokee, Okla.
250-Marie L. De Laskey, 496 Bellevue Ave.,
Winthrop, Mass.
251-Ann Soltis, 12308 Saywell Ave., 8144124
Cleveland 8, Ohio
252-Mrs. Bertha M. Lloyd, 307 W. 7th St.,
W.....ing, Ill.
253-Mrs. Bertha Liebhart, Box 221,
Canoga Park, Calif.
254-Mrs. Louis A. Prillmayer, 805 Oak St.,
Quincy, Ill.
255-Maude Oaks,G.D. Springfield, Mo.
256-Miss Cora Cripps, RR5,Cullman, Ala.
257-Mrs. Carrie Tolson, RR 2, Box 72,
Clay City, Ky.
258-Mrs. Lou Lawson, RR 2, Hohenwald, Tenn.
259-Mrs. Annie M. Carr, 108 Covington St.,
Montgomery, Ala.
260-Mrs. Thelma Kosh, 4341 W. 106th St.,
Inglewood, Calif.
261-Mrs. Bertha Conover,Box 13, Cuba, Ohio.
262-Mrs. Gloria Clare Holden, P. O. Box
177, S.S. Station, Springfield, Mo.
263-Mrs. E. Clark, 2705 Midway St.,
Shreveport, La.
264-Mrs. Helen Case, 1480 Cleveland Ave.,
Columbus 3, Ohio.
265-Grace L. Miller, 132 W. Territorial
Road, Battle Creek, Mich.
266-Miss Mary Baron, 87 N. Center St.,
Youngstown 8, Ohio.
267-Canceled.
268-Canceled.
269Mrs. Lois Hamelberg, 1666 North
California Ave., Chicago 47, Ill.
270-Alice Luttrell, Box 29, Pumpkin
Chapel, Ky.
271-Ruby Weir, 903 Shady St.#9
Columbus, Miss.
272-Jean Haley, Lock Box 803, Sioux City,
Iowa.
273-Miss Ruth Helms, RR 5, Box 234,
Monroe, La.
274-Sebe Prine, RR 3, Box 225,
Columbus, Miss.
275-Mrs. Frances Rogers, 2717 E. 1st St.,
Fort Worth, Texas.

276-Mrs. J. B. Carren, Clarence, Iowa.
276-Mrs. Lillian Reerewoer, 1947 Julian
Ave., San Diego, Calif.
278-Grace Crowder, 2514 N. Water St.,
Bay City, Mich.
279-Mrs. Doris Beatty, 514 Page St.,
Fort Worth, Texas.
280-Mrs. Martha De Mamphrey, Box 154,
Lawrence, Nebr.
281-Mrs. Lena Murphy, Lupus, Mo.
282-Jane Stewart, Sparrow, Ky.,
283-Pearl E. Ward, 713 Ohio Ave.,
East St. Louis, Ill.
284-Dolores Smart, 1 Spruce St., #
Biddeford, Maine.
285-canceled.
286-Josephine Salzman, 922 Maple St.,
Conshchocken, Pa.
287-Uliste Mills, 646 Preston St.,
Paintsville, Ky.
288-Mrs. Leora Nelson, 4847 Raiger Ave.,
Dallas 14, Texas.
289-Mrs. Myra Johnson, 809 N. 3rd St.,
Fredonia, Kans.
290-Mrs. Dorine Olsen, 1132 N. Platte
Ave., Fremont, Nebr.
291-Elizabeth Harrison, 6681 Drexel Ave.,
Los Angeles 36, Calif.
292-Bertha Jane Gee, RR 4, Cleveland, Tenn.
293-Mrs. Mindie J. Kerley, Simpson, Ill.
294-Lydia Bryant, Box 92, Custer, Mich.
295-Mrs. Ruth Russell, 6616 Beecmont
Ave., Cincinnati, Ohio.
296-Mrs. Nancy M. Stone, 326 E. Hannum
St., Carterville, Mo.
297-Mrs. Harriett A. Withrow, 240 Raymer
Blvd., Toledo, Ohio.
298-Jane Gelding, Galax, Va.
299-Nancy O'Shaughnessy, 1606 Saint
Mark Sq., Philadelphia, Pa.
300-Eleanor Anne Reid, 815 'S' Ave.,
Springfield, Mo.
301-Elizabeth Melniva, P. O. Box 33,
Manitowoc, Wis.
302-Mary Boyer, Lake Ozark, Mo.
303-Martha Brader, 2124 Birch St.,
Easton, Pa.

304-Belle Pittman, 248 S. Michigan Ave.,
Wellston, Ohio.
305-Mrs. Lavada Wharton, 413 Ogden Ave.,
Bastrop, La.
306-Mary C. McPherson, 804 S. Governer
St. Evansville, Ind.
307-Gertrude Thompson, 720 W. 9th St.,
Buena Park, Calif.
308-Mrs. Anna Hamelau, RR 2, Box 64,
Winnebago, Minn.
309-Mrs. Grace Burleson, 501 Preusser
St., San Angelo, Texas.
310-Nora White, Box 485, West Plaine, Mo.
311-Mrs. Dana Carver, RR 1, Mount Juliet,
Tenn.
312-Mary Hannstein, 1115 Jefferson St.,
Saint Charles, Mo.
313-Florence M. Sarell, Oakland, N. J.
314-Clara McKennan, P. O. Box 1996,
Mojave, Calif.
315-Mrs. Minnie Rouze, 407 E. Rogers St.,
Valdosta, Ga.
316-Ada M. Martin, P. O. Box 155,
Galena Park, Texas.
317-Mrs. Frances Ketchum, Box 9,
Hillsboro, Texas.
318-Ida M. Bloodgood, 3311 S. Grand Ave.,
Los Angeles 7, Calif.
319-Mrs. Nancy Garrett, Gainesville
Route, West Plains, Mo.
320-Mrs. M. E. Hanson, 12 Wood St.,
Council Grove, Kans.
321-Miss Irene Moreland, RR 1, Box 184-A,
Morgantown, W. Va.
322-Miss Margaret Bernard, 516 - 5th St.,
Traverse City, Mich.
323-Neola Creger, Dakota City, Nebr.
324-Mrs. Georgia Taylor, 906 Liberty
St. El Dorado, Ark.
325-Freda Burkett, RR 3, %E. W. Kaler,
Meadville, Pa.
326-Laura Lutes, Vada, Ky.
327-Ella Daylong, Carlsbad, N. Mex.
328-Mrs. Eduna Novak, RR 2, Box 124,
Medford, Wis.
329-Ollie Elms, RR 3, Rusk, Texas.
330-Mrs. Onie Mills, RR 1, Winfield, Ala.

331—Elizabeth Day, 615 W. Noble,
Oklahoma City, Okla.
332—Mrs. Nellie Knight, 1516 Sherman
St., Marinette, Wis.
333—Mrs. Laura Mast, RR 1, Farmington,
Iowa.
334—Miss Julia Graham, 206 - 8th St.,
Bowling Green, Ky.,
335—Mrs. Clara Westcott, RR 3, Box 543,
Hillsboro, Oregon.
336—Harriette Hughes, Box 814,
Bryan, Texas.
337—Irene Elberfeld, 10 Cleveland Ave.,
Tonawanda, N. Y.
338—Bertha A. King, 2134 N. W. Flanders
St., Portland 10, Oregon.
339—Canceled.
340—Mrs. Elizabeth Bergen, Elbing, Kans.
341—Maude McGarvey, 507 Porter St.,
Alton, Ill.
342—Mildred L. Crawford, RR 2, Box 261,
Monroe, La.
343—Genevieve C. Steinbarge, 193 Howard
Ave., Roosevelt, N. Y.
344—Nettie Fetterroff, Douglass, Kans.

PLEASE NOTICE—Names Omitted or penciled have been canceled.

DEVOTED TO THE INTERESTS OF THE UNMARRIED

The Exchange

No. 344

PUBLISHED BY THE

EXCHANGE CLUB KANSAS CITY, MO.

3827 Main Street, Kansas City, Mo.
Established in 1909

A MEDIUM FOR THE INTRODUCTION OF

MATRIMONIALLY INCLINED LADIES AND GENTLEMEN

MAKE YOUR OWN SELECTIONS

Two Dollars pays for the name and address of every lady given in this Catalogue. You make the selections yourself from this list of descriptions. The published descriptions contain full information in regard to the ladies, their age, religion, personal appearance, means, value of property, etc.

The original descriptions are always on file in our office. The full names and addresses of the ladies will be sent you by return mail in a plain envelope on receipt of $2.00. Send your orders now and be one of the first to correspond.

1—Considered very attractive, a neat dresser, have a quiet disposition, easy to get along with. Am a good cook and housekeeper. My favorite sports are bowling, horseback riding and dancing. Have some talent in music, play a guitar. English, Christian, common school education, age 20, dark hair, blue eyes, fair complexion, ht. 5-7, wt. 122. See my photo above.

2—I am a widow, a retired nurse living on my farm, very lonely. Have a kind disposition, everyone I meet likes me, make friends easily. Am just plain, nice looking. American, Christian, common school education, age 45, black hair, brown eyes, olive complexion, ht. 5-2, wt. 100. Wish to hear from one near my age, likes home life.

3—I make a good appearance, dress reasonably well but not extravagantly, and try to adjust myself in a reasonable way, concerning most things. My specialty is my home and its environments, cooking, planning meals, etc. American, Presbyterian, high school and business college education, secretary, age 35, chestnut brown hair, blue-grey eyes, fair complexion, ht. 5-3, wt. 106. Worth $4000.

4—I am a widow by death, like sports, dancing, good music, a nice home, flowers and pets, like to play cards and entertain. Have a nice appearance, dress neatly, fair looking. German, Catholic, common school education, age 52, light brown hair, blue eyes, fair complexion, ht. 5-5, wt. 120. Own home and car. Interested in someone congenial, 55 to 60.

5—Have always been considered very neat and stylish in appearance. I enjoy traveling, camping and fishing, also like a good show. Irish-American, Methodist, college educated, age 59, light hair, blue eyes, fair complexion, ht. 5-5, wt. 145. Own property and oil interests. Would like to hear from a gentleman 60 to 70.

6—I am friendly and jolly, like sports, fond of country life. My friends say I look like I have plenty of money, according to the way I dress. American, Baptist, common school education, nice looking, age 58, brown slightly grey hair, brown eyes, good complexion, ht. 5-2½, wt 140. Own 52 acre farm. Would like to hear from a farmer of neat appearance.

80 | Wendell Affield

7—I am very reasonable about everything, have lots of patience, and am of a pleasant disposition. Have been told I am young looking for my age. American, English descent, protestant, fair education, age 47, brown hair and eyes, medium fair complexion, ht. 5-6, wt. 155. Some means. Wish to hear from a jolly, home loving type of gentleman.

8—Always appear presentable, stylish dresser, well formed, trim figure, young in appearance, active and quick mentally and physically, very even disposition, versatile. American, protestant, college education, dietitician, age 42, medium blonde hair, blue eyes, fair complexion, blonde type, ht. 5-4, wt. 135. Worth $5000, will inherit.

9—I am considered a good woman and neighbor, love to attend church services. Am not ashamed to present myself in any place. American, protestant, good education, age 58, grey hair, blue eyes, fair complexion, ht. 5-6, wt. 170. Own home. Wish to hear from an honest, reliable farmer, pleasant disposition, one near my own age.

10—I am a very quiet, affectionate lady, like to make other people happy. Considered nice looking and near appearing. American, Baptist, fair education, a nurse, age 57, auburn hair, light brown eyes, fair complexion, ht. 5-6, wt. 180. Own small farm and home. Would like to correspond with a kind, sober man, 50 to 65, one that would be interested in a home.

11—Very neat appearing and nice looking, not a flashy dresser, but stylish. Am good natured, like to fish, hunt, travel, love children, a good cook and housekeeper. American, protestant, fair education, age 40, light brown hair, grey eyes, fair complexion, blonde type, ht. 5-5½, wt. 145. Own two houses. Matrimony in view if suited.

12—Excellent cook and housekeeper, kind disposition, neat appearing, pleasing and sociable. American, Christian, common school education, seamstress, age 50, brown hair, blue eyes, very fair complexion, ht. 5-5, wt. 165. Own home. Would like to correspond with a Christian gentleman, a lover of home life, wants a real pal.

13—I am honest, sincere, truthful, broadminded, and like to meet others that are the same way. I have a gentle disposition, but have strong will power. American, Presbyterian, grade school education, age 33, dark brown hair, grey eyes, medium fair complexion, ht. 5-2, wt. 122. Own a small farm. Desire a Christian companion, honest and sincere.

14—I have hosts of friends, and have a good reputation in the community where I live. Considered nice looking, have a jolly disposition, full of fun. American, Methodist, grammer school education, age 53, light brown hair, hazel eyes, good complexion, ht. 5-2, wt. 115. Own my home. The one of my choice must be of good morals, no bad habits.

15—Have good habits, able to fit in any place socially, not a gossip. Fairly good looking, neat in appearance, good disposition, experienced housekeeper and cook. American, high school education, typist, age 50, grey hair, medium fair complexion, grey eyes, ht. 5-5, wt. 135. Some means. Desire a companion of moderate habits.

16—I love a nice home, and am very neat about my work, a good cook and housekeeper. I have some talent in music, play violin. American, Methodist, common school education, age 37, dark hair, blue-grey eyes, very fair complexion, brunette type, ht. 5-3, wt. 138. Own my home. Would like to hear from a gentleman that likes home life.

17—Neat appearing, very attractive, a good mixer, can do most any kind of work, especially in cooking and keeping house. American, protestant, grade school education, age 49, brown partly grey hair, brown eyes, olive complexion, ht. 5-2, wt. 135, good figure. Own home in town and 320 acre farm. Wish to hear from a man of business ability.

18—Widow by death, jolly, pleasant disposition, neat appearance, nice looking, a member of Baptist Church, Eastern Star, Rebekahs. American, high school education, age 64, partly grey hair, fair complexion, grey eyes, ht. 5-4, wt. 143. Own a five room modern home. No objection to a poor man, if he is worthy and a good, moral man.

19—Am kind hearted and honest, make friends, associate with the best class. Am a widow, living alone, considered nice looking. American, Baptist, common school education, age 53, brown hair, blue eyes, fair complexion, ht. 5-5, wt. 140. Have some means. Would like to hear from a man of good habits, age about 50 to 60.

20—I am considered good looking, have a happy disposition, dress plain but good, and always well dressed. French-American, Catholic, well educated, age 54, dark brown hair and

eyes, very light complexion, ht. 5-3, wt. 188. Own apartment house valued at $6000, will inherit $10,000. Wish to hear from a quiet type of man, good habits.

21—Have lived on a farm most of my life, a good citizen, come from good family. Considered nice looking, neat appearing, well groomed. American, Christian, high school education, age 31, brown hair, hazel eyes, fair complexion, ht. 5-4, wt. 125. Some means. Wish to hear from a Christian, honest with himself and fellow man.

22—I am considered fair looking, good natured and jolly, a good worker. I like house work, also outdoor work such as gardening and raising poultry. American, Methodist, grade school education, age 58, dark hair, grey eyes, light complexion, ht. 5-3, wt. 142. Own six room bungalow and $10,000 worth of personal property. Lonely, seeking a good companion.

23—Am just another lonesome widow, sensible in all things, easy to get along with, like to travel, go to a show once in awhile, have lots of friends, rather nice looking. American, common school education, age 55, brown hair and eyes, fair complexion, ht. 5-5, wt. 123. Own six room house and garage. Willing to go 50-50 in all things.

24—Am a good housekeeper, very neat appearing, wear nice clothes, good natured and jolly, love a home, like all clean sports, wonderful personality. Welsh, Baptist; high school education, age 63, brown hair, blue eyes, light complexion, ht. 5-6, wt. 160. Own my home. Wish to hear from rancher, or any good, honest man, 55 to 65 years of age.

25—I am very fond of a nice home, like to keep house and cook. Considered nice looking, dress well and make a nice appearance. Am of a jolly, pleasant disposition, make friends easily. American, common school education, age 18, brown hair and eyes, fair complexion, brunette type, ht. 5-4, wt. 125, neat figure. Wish to hear from a young man 18 to 25. See my photo above.

26—Am a widow by death, no children, like to cook and keep house, enjoy sports, shows, do not smoke or drink, considered neat appearing. Swedish-American, Methodist, tenth grade school education, age 48, blonde hair, blue eyes, fair complexion, blonde type, ht. 5-5, wt. 160. Own a farm, house and car. Wish to hear from a gentleman 45 to 55 years of age.

27—Am a lonely young lady, a lover of home and children, good disposition, like to work, held same position for 14 years. Considered average looking, neat appearing, dress well. American, fair education, age 38, dark brown hair, brown eyes, medium fair complexion, ht. 5-5, wt. 125. Worth $2000.

Wish to hear from a home loving gentleman, fair looking, 36 to 45.

28—I am a widow by death, entirely alone, no near relatives, very lonely. Am always neat appearing, very precise about my surroundings and home. American, golden rule religion, commercial school education, market gardener, age 55, dark brown greying hair, blue eyes, fair complexion, ht. 5-5, wt. 150. Own my home. Wish to hear from one trustworthy and honest.

29—I am considered attractive and nice looking, have a sunny disposition, well experienced in all household duties. English and Irish descent, Baptist, fair education, age 41, brown hair and eyes, ht. 5-4, wt. 135, nice figure, I own my home and a farm of 53 acres. Would like a companion capable of taking care of a farm, no drinker, in good health.

30—I love to make garden and raise poultry, and have always had the best of luck with such work. Have always had good health and am considered young looking for my age. German and Irish descent, fair education, age 65, brown and grey hair, blue eyes, light complexion, ht. 5-3, wt. 125. Own my home. Prefer a farmer, as I have lived in country until lately.

31—I am a widow by death, no children, and find it a very lonely life living alone on a farm. Considered good looking, kind and affectionate, neat in appearance, a home lover. American, protestant, occupation farming, age 56, brown and grey hair, blue eyes, fair complexion, ht. 5-4, wt. 160. Own a farm, stock, etc., worth $14,000. Desire companion neat appearing, industrious.

32—I have a good, honest name, and can give best of reference. I have a very pleasing disposition, considered nice looking. Farmerette, fair education, age 32, brown hair, blue eyes, fair complexion, ht. 4-10, wt. 159. I own a good farm with good buildings, also a store on highway. Would like to hear from a gentleman 35 to 40, a good worker.

mrs alvina callahan
Turkey Ky.

33—I have a jolly disposition, like lots of clean fun and amusement, but do love home life, and am a good manager. Norwegian, Lutheran, common school education, age 48, auburn hair, hazel eyes, fair complexion, ht. 5-7, wt. 148. Own property worth around $5000. Would like to correspond with someone honest and dependable, near my own age and height.

34—I am a widow woman by death, no children, kind hearted, pleasant and congenial. American, fair education, age 55, have brown hair mingled with grey, blue eyes, fair complexion, ht. 5-4, wt. 160. I own a farm and car, and have some other means. I would like to correspond with a worthy gentleman, age 55 to 60, and prefer one with no children.

35—Good natured, always smiling, have a fine personality. Am rather small, but not thin, rather nice figure, considered fair looking. American, Christian, high school graduate, first class cook and housekeeper, age 60, dark brown slightly grey hair, blue eyes, olive complexion, ht. 5-3, wt. 100. Have some means. Prefer a companion that is jolly.

36—I am a widow by death, work for a living, have good business experience in different lines, can fit in any place. American, protestant, high school education, age 59, greying hair, brown eyes, fair complexion, wt. 100. Would like to correspond with a gentleman that is honest and upright, considerate, no bad habits. Own my home.

37—Considered very young looking for age, very active, look nice in my clothes, good character, mild disposition, no bad habits, a widow by death, all alone. Scotch-Irish, protestant, high school education, age 50, dark brown hair and eyes, olive complexion, ht. 5-6, wt. 165. Worth $10,000 in property. Wish to hear from any good man 55 to 60.

38—I try to be helpful, especially to the sick and shut-ins. Considered of outstanding character, very neat appearing, sunny disposition, rather nice looking. American, Methodist, fair education, taught school, age 51, brown hair, dark blue eyes, very fair complexion, ht. 5-3, wt. 145. Own home, have income. Am a widow by divorce, have talent in music, sing, play piano.

39—I have been a widow by death for the past ten years, have four sons, three married, one in the service, so I am alone and lonesome. Have a good disposition, good cook and housekeeper. American, fair education, age 48, partly grey hair, brown eyes, fair complexion, ht. 5-5, wt. 142. Own a home. Wish to hear from someone that is respectable.

40—People say that I have an attractive personality, a good figure, and considered intelligent and witty. American, Methodist, two years college education, stenographer, age 48, auburn hair, blue eyes, fair complexion, ht. 5-7, wt. 140. Have means. I would like to correspond with a Christian gentleman, a companionable, home loving man.

41—I am neat appearing, good dresser, nice looking, good cook and housekeeper, like, and enjoy a good home. American, protestant, high school education, age 50, brown some grey hair, grey eyes, fair complexion, ht. 5-5, wt. 135. Have some means. Would like to correspond with a gentleman not over 60, nice looking, no children, good disposition.

42—Considered fair looking, nice appearance, good disposition, well experienced in cooking and keeping house, like to work, keep busy, like to travel, out for a good time. American, Baptist, fair education, business lady, age 43, dark brown hair, brown eyes, fair complexion, ht. 5-7, wt. 169. Worth $4000, have two trucks and a car. Wish to hear from a business man.

43—I have a very pleasant, affectionate disposition, considered nice looking, very neat appearance, nicely dressed, a widow by death, no children, a very good cook and housekeeper. American, high school education, a nurse, age 53, brown hair and eyes, fair complexion, ht. 5-4, wt. 120, neat figure. Own real estate worth $4500. Admire men with dark hair and eyes.

44—I am a quiet, religious, industrious person, associate with the best of people, considered nice looking and dress well. Am a hotel operator, wonderful cook and housekeeper. American, protestant, well educated, ex-teacher, age 45, dark brown hair, blue eyes, fair complexion, ht. 5-5, wt. 137. Own my home. Wish to hear from an honest, industrious gentleman.

46—I have a good personality, pleasant, well mannered, well liked by neighbors, school and church groups, belong to parent teachers association, average appearance, fair looking. American, protestant, junior high school education, age 36, brown hair and eyes, fair complexion, brunette, ht. 5-1, wt. 100. I own my home and some livestock.

45—I enjoy swimming, riding, camping and outdoor life. I also like the movies, reading, the radio. Considered rather nice looking, a good, neat, tasty dresser. French-Canadian, Catholic, high school and commercial education, age 26, brown hair, blue eyes, medium fair complexion, ht. 5-6½, wt. 135. Interested in a young man of fair education. See my photo above.

47—I am a widow by death, considered very good looking, a good cook and housekeeper, have a very good disposition. American, Baptist, common school education, age 42, dark brown hair and eyes, olive complexion, ht. 5-2, wt. 115. Own a five room bungalow, fair income. Would like to hear from gentleman about my own age, dark hair and eyes.

48—I enjoy all outdoor sports, especially fishing. I drive my own car, like music, sing and dance, have jolly disposition, considered nice looking, well dressed. German-American, Catholic, grammar school education, age 48, brown hair, blue eyes, fair complexion, ht. 5-7, wt. 150, nice figure. Have some means. I admire the tall type.

49—I am considered to have a very neat and pleasing appearance. Have a good disposition, no temper, like a good time. American, French descent, high school education, office worker, age 38, brown hair and eyes, fair complexion, brunette type, good looking, ht. 5-4, wt. 130, slender figure. Own my home. Desire companion that is jolly and full of fun.

50—I am a fairly good looking woman for one of my years, and perfectly healthy. Am living alone and need the help of someone, as I have a big place here, and could with some help make a good living. American, Baptist, good education, age 57, brown and grey hair, brown eyes, fair complexion, ht. 5-4, wt. 132. I own my home.

51—I am very industrious in my home, a good cook and housekeeper, have a good position, but should I marry, prefer housekeeping altogether. Am considered attractive, have a jolly disposition. American, protestant, grammar school education, age 36, brown hair, grey eyes, fair complexion, ht. 5-1, wt. 104, neat figure. Own my home and car.

52—I am a widow by death, a good, Christian woman, considered rather nice looking and have a nice appearance, a very good cook and housekeeper. American, Methodist, fair education, age 62, brown and grey hair, blue eyes, fair complexion, ht. 5-3, wt. 140. Own my home. Would like to correspond with a gentleman my age or older, one of good habits.

53—My friends say that I dress well and am nice looking, and have a good personality. I am a widow of a physician, no dependents, very lonely. American, protestant, two years college education, laboratory and X-ray Technician, age 47, brown hair, grey eyes, fair complexion, ht. 5-7, wt. 175. Own about $10,000 worth of real estate.

54—I have many compliments on my personal appearance, considered neat and attractive. American, protestant, common school education, age 50, blonde hair, blue eyes, fair complexion, ht. 5-2½, wt. 135, good figure. I own a nice home. The one of my choice need not be wealthy, as money does not buy happiness, but should have some means and willing to work.

55—Am a widow by death, very young looking, no children, my disposition is very good. I like the open spaces, do not like to be in doors. American, common school education, age 46, black hair, dark grey eyes, olive complexion, ht. 5-2, wt. 110. Am worth $10,000, consisting of nine room brick house and 96 acres of land. Would like to hear from ranchers or farmers.

56—I am well known where I live and well liked, can furnish the best of reference. Am good natured, love music, neat appearing, ambitious, have traveled, a good business woman. American, French and English descent, age 45, brown hair, dark brown eyes, fair, healthy complexion, ht. 5-5, wt. 125. Have means, operate apartment. Interested in a good, moral gentleman.

57—I have been a widow for the past ten years, and am very lonesome for a companion and help-mate. Considered nice looking and young appearing for age. American, Unitarian, fair education, age 64, black and grey hair, black eyes, good complexion, ht. 5-1, wt. 138. I own a good home and have a small income. Desire a companion able to pay household expenses.

58—Neat appearing, good personality, refined, treat all with courtesy, but select friends rather slowly and cautiously. Am a widow by death, a good cook and housekeeper. American, protestant, high school education, age 45, brown hair and eyes, medium fair complexion, ht. 5-5, wt. 140. Own four unit apartment building and five room house.

59—Am a home lover, a neat housekeeper and good, plain cook, a hard worker, neat appearing, do not have any bad habits, like to camp, fish and hunt. I am a widow, age 54, brown slightly grey hair, hazel eyes, ht. 5-8, wt. 185. Own my home, have stock and chickens. Am seeking a companion near my age or older, a farm man, kind and affectionate.

60—I am a widow by divorce, have one little eight years of age. My friends consider me nice looking and of neat appearance. American, protestant, common school education, age 31, blonde hair, grey eyes, fair complexion, blonde type, ht. 5-1, wt. 87. Have some means. Would like to correspond with a gentleman that is nice, intelligent, need not be rich.

Mrs. Sible Massey Boy 333
Naples Tex

61—Am a widow by death, passably nice looking, neat appearance, have a kind, unselfish disposition, good housekeeper and plain cook. American, protestant, fair education, saleslady and practical nurse, age 50, brown hair and eyes, fair complexion, ht. 5-7, wt. 160. Have some means. Want a companion of good, sound judgment, jolly disposition.

63—I am a widow by death, good housekeeper and cook, good, pleasant disposition, dignified, called very good looking by friends. American, protestant, high school education, nurse, age 42, dark brown and grey hair, blue eyes, very fair complexion, ht. 5-2, wt.

160. I own a six room house, well furnished. Wish to hear from one clean in mind and body.

62—My friends say I look very nice in my clothes, and that I am always very neat appearing. I have a very pleasing disposition, considered nice looking, can cook and keep house. Irish descent, eighth grade education, clerk in store, age 18, black hair, blue eyes, fair complexion, ht. 5-4, wt. 113. Would like to hear from a nice looking young man, a neat dresser. See my photo above.

64—I am of good character, good natured, rather nice looking, very congenial and likeable, a good housekeeper and cook. American, protestant, fair education, age 46, auburn hair, brown eyes, light complexion, ht. 5-3½, wt. 160. Own a home. Would like to correspond with a nice, refined gentleman, kind, affectionate disposition, age 46 to 55.

65—I am a perfect lady in every respect, do not associate with bad company, do not drink or dance, a widow by death, neat appearing. American, common school education, age 62, grey hair, blue eyes, fair complexion, ht. 5-2, wt. 135. Have fair amount of means. Would like to hear from a real gentleman, no drunkard or gambler, a home lover.

66—I am a widow by death, considered fair looking, a very neat person, not glamorous, but like to look my best at all times. Scotch-Irish descent, protestant, common school education, age 32, brown hair and eyes, olive complexion, brunette type, ht. 5-9½, wt. 195. Own my home. Would have no objection to a widower with one or two small children.

67—I am alone and very lonely, have worked hard all my life, very industrious, like nice things and keep them nice. American, common school education, age 63, brown slightly grey hair, light complexion, grey eyes, ht. 5-1, wt. 95. Own a farm and three houses I rent. Would like to hear from a farmer, as I farm and need the help of a good man.

68—Am considered very nice looking, neat dresser, love the homey things of life, such as cooking, keeping house, poultry raising, gardening, etc. Am musically inclined, play piano and sing. American, protestant, age 33, medium brown hair, large dark grey eyes, ht. 5-6, wt. 140, well proportioned. I own city property, also acreage, income and other means.

69—I love all outdoor sports, hunting and fishing especially, also horseback riding. I am all alone, have no children, very lonely for companionship. Am not bad looking, have a sunny disposition, full of life. Irish, high school education, age 47, brown hair and eyes, light complexion, ht. 4-10, wt. 122. I own a small rabbit and poultry ranch, will inherit three ranches.

70—Versatile, unencumbered business woman and home maker, strong and healthy, vegetarian, do not use tobacco or intoxicants, love the simple things and know what it takes to make life happy and living worth while. American, college education, age 46, brown hair, grey eyes, olive complexion, ht. 5-4, wt. 128, well proportioned. Some means. Prefer to hear from middle aged gentlemen.

71—I have lived alone for two years on the farm, can do any kind of work, and am a real farmer. I have a cheerful disposition, do not nag or fuss. A good business woman, buy and sell stock. Scotch-Irish, Methodist, common school education, age 52, dark brown hair, blue eyes, medium fair complexion, ht. 5-2, wt. 160. Want someone willing to help on the farm.

72—Am a widow, pleasant disposition, home loving, no bad habits, like to keep house, cook and sew, neat appearing, fair looking. I love to do kind deeds for other people. American, protestant, fair education, age 55, grey hair, fair complexion, grey eyes, ht. 5-4, wt. 113. Am worth several thousand dollars. Wish to hear from one near my own age, kind and home loving.

73—Would have no objection to a poor man if he proves himself worthy and industrious. I have a kind and affectionate disposition, considered very young looking for my age. American, protestant, age 70, brown and grey hair, blue eyes, medium fair complexion, ht. 5-6, wt. 148. Am raising poultry, own a small farm and city property. Desire someone that could come here to live.

74—Am of a settled nature, energetic, trustworthy, neat appearing and considered good looking, have a stately, alert appearance. American, German descent, Catholic, high school graduate, living on farm, age 34, auburn hair, hazel eyes, fair complexion, blonde type, ht. 5-5, wt. 160. Own a farm and two houses. Prefer correspondents from 40 to 45, farmers or business men.

88 | Wendell Affield

75—Am a divorcee, no children or other relatives, quiet and good natured, love travel and outdoor life, camping, fishing, etc. Am usually admired for my neat personal appearance. American, protestant, two years college education, nurse, age 65, grey hair, blue eyes, fair complexion, ht. 5-5, wt. 175. Worth about $5000. Wish to hear from one that is refined, home loving, affectionate.

76—Considered fine looking, look much younger than my age, fine carriage, keep abreast of the times, a home lover. American, Christian, high school and business education, ex-school teacher, postmaster for thirteen years, age 65, iron grey hair, dark blue eyes, very fair complexion, ht. 5-5, wt. 150. Own 400 acres of land, have stock on one of my farms.

77—Have a happy, cheerful disposition, excellent cook and housekeeper. I am able to earn an independent living and put aside a nice little sum each year. American, protestant, high school and business college education, bookkeeper, age 57, dark hair, dark blue eyes, fair complexion, ht. 5-4, wt. 145, nice figure. Have an independent living.

78—Widow by death, considered by some to be good looking. I do dress nice and take lots of pride in making a nice appearance. American, protestant, common school education, occupation farming. Age 50, brown hair, blue eyes, fair complexion, ht. 5-6, wt. 130. Have means. Would like to hear from a neat appearing gentleman, no bad habits, good disposition.

79—Am a widow, no dependents, nice looking for my age. My entire interest is in my home, like to keep it clean. I am of good character, do not smoke, drink or play cards. American, Baptist, common school education, age 55, brown hair and eyes,

medium fair complexion, ht. 5-2, wt. 130. Have plenty of means to live on. Would like a worthwhile companion.

80—I am tall and slender, considered good looking, very neat and attractive. Am good natured, very good sense of humor, like to read and study. German, protestant, high school education, a nurse, age 40, dark brown hair, brown eyes, olive complexion, brunette, ht. 5-6½, wt. 135. Have some means. I feel I have the training to fulfill the duties in most any home.

81—Considered a very nice girl, have lots of friends, no bad habits, keep good company, also a good Christian, fair education, farmer girl, age 18, dark brown hair, brown eyes, fair complexion, ht. 5-5, wt. 116, slender figure. Would like to correspond with a young man of fair education, one in business, or one that likes farm life. See my photo above.

althea Hughes Sous valley
marietta aflea R/.

82—Am very conservative and economical, efficient in every way. Considered far above the average in personal appearance, dress well, have a good personality, kind and considerate. American, Baptist, high school education, farm lady, age 48, dark brown hair and eyes, good complexion, ht. 5-9, wt. 195. I own a 160 acre farm. Wish to hear from business man or farmer.

83—Am a widow by death, a good, Christian lady, honest and truthful, have good health, look much younger than my age, a good housekeeper and cook. American, Presbyterian, high school education, age 58, mixed grey hair, fair complexion, grey eyes, ht. 5-6, wt. 158. Own a small farm. Would like to hear from a man that is truthful, and honest, some means.

84—I am young looking for my age, could pass for 40 or 45. I am neatly formed, and attractive in appearance. German and Irish descent, age 56, natural wavy brown hair, ht. 5-3, wt. 142. I enjoy all outdoor sports. Would like a companion that enjoys country life. I have farm property, a car and other means. Am all alone. Would like someone near my own age.

85—Am alone, good disposition, always smiling, considerate, have personality, very neat, full of pep, quick and alert. American, protestant, fair education, age 50, auburn and grey hair, brown eyes, light complexion, ht. 5-2, wt. 135, neat figure. Worth $5000 in bonds. Would like to hear from a gentleman older than myself, one who likes outdoor life and work.

86—Am a Christian worker, a bible teacher, have a common school education, plus business experience, also a practical nurse, a good personality. American, Baptist, age 50, dark brown hair and eyes, medium fair complexion, ht. 5-4, wt. 165. Own 80 acre farm. Would consider a poor man if of good character, intelligent, with business ability.

87—Am a widow by death, well liked by friends and neighbors, pleasant disposition, fair looking, well experienced in household duties. American, Christian, fair education, age 42, brown hair and eyes, medium fair complexion, brunette type, ht. 5-7, wt. 162. Own my home, a five room house and two lots. No objection to a poor man if willing to do his part.

88—I do not drink or smoke, but I do like to be sociable with people, and do like company and good times. I have a good disposition, considered neat appearing. English-American, good education, age 34, dark auburn hair, hazel eyes, very fair complexion, ht. 5-4. Worth $10,000. Would like to correspond with a view to matrimony. No objection to a poor man.

89—Am a widow by death, well respected, a nice, honest person, easy to get along with. I love farming, and live on a farm, but am very lonely. American, Baptist, common school education, age 53, partly grey hair, brown eyes, fair complexion, ht. 5-4, wt. 147. Have some means. I want a good, honest, industrious companion, one that likes farm life.

90—Am a widow alone, no children, have a jolly, good disposition, good mixer, love clean fun, good cook and housekeeper, good health, love outdoor life. Was raised on a farm and like farm life. American, protestant, common school education, practical nurse, age 53, brown and grey hair, blue eyes, fair complexion, ht. 5-5, wt. 176. Own property. Will marry if suited.

91—Am a good manager and worker, economical, a good cook and housekeeper, make money, have some means, own my little farm. Considered good looking, have a kind disposition, easy to get along with. English, common school education, religious, age 48, dark brown hair, dark eyes, fair complexion, ht. 5-3, wt. 165. Desire a companion that is fair looking, kind disposition.

92—I am a lover of home life, like housework and cooking. People say I am nice looking, and that I dress well and make a nice appearance. I have a very pleasant disposition, like good, clean fun. American, Lutheran, age 45, dark greying hair, light complexion, ht. 5-6, wt. 158. Own home. Would like to hear from a steady worker, one who would like to share my nice home.

93—Am in the best of health, love clean sports and social life. Am attractive and dress in good taste, good disposition, an affectionate person, a fine home maker. American, Jewish, high school education, saleslady, age 43, black hair, black eyes, fair complexion, brunette type, ht. 5-3, wt. 148. Worth $2500. Wish to hear from a business man, age 50 to 55, in good health.

94—Widow by divorce, dress neat and in good taste, but not elaborate, really enjoy cooking and keeping house. I am a forelady in shoe factory, held this position for last four years. American, protestant, common school education, age 43, light brown hair, blue eyes, fair complexion, ht. 5-2, wt. 110. Own my home. Prefer a home lover, good worker, nice looking.

95—Can get along with anyone, likeable personality, make friends quickly and easily. I am neat appearing, nice slender figure, wear my clothes well and know how to dress. American, Baptist, well educated, insurance lady, age 40, black hair, grey eyes, fair complexion, ht. 5-4, wt. 125. Worth $8,000. Wish to hear from someone near my age, a good manager.

96—I do not want to say I am good looking, but my friends say I look as if I was only 40. I have a nice home in the city, and a nice country home where I am living at present time. American, protestant, good education, age 50, brown greying hair, blue eyes, fair complexion, ht. 5-4, wt. 160. Desire a nice companion that can attend to business, and can be a home man.

97—Am a good manager and business woman, even temperament, a very pleasing personality, have trav-

eled extensively. Considered good looking and a neat dresser. Have lots of good qualities. American, protestant, junior high school education, business woman, age 39, dark brown hair, brown eyes, fair complexion, brunette, ht. 5-8, wt. 210. Own my own business, fair income.

98—I am a widow, splendid health, own nice property, good education, well accomplished and self made. I am attractive, do not look my age, and always very ambitious and full of life. American, Baptist, part college education, a nurse, age 45, brown hair and eyes, olive complexion, ht. 5-4, wt. 145. Have property and money. Wish to hear from gentleman 45 to 50.

100—Was raised on a farm, but like being in town better, although it would not matter where I lived just so I found the right one. Am considered fairly nice looking, have a good, pleasant disposition. American, Presbyterian, high school education, saleslady age 25, brown hair, grey eyes, fair complexion, ht. 5-11, wt. 148. Wish to hear from young men of suitable age. See my photo above.

agnes warner Box 1134
Salina Kans.

mattie Van Dusen
710 Berger St.
malvern ark.

99—Have a good personality, easy to get along with, no bad habits, very neat appearing, considered nice looking, well experienced in household duties. American, Christian, common school education, age 38, dark blonde hair, blue eyes, fair complexion, ht. 5-7, wt. 165. Own my own home. Wish to hear from a Christian, nice looking, good personality, need not be rich.

101—I am just a good, honest lady and want to meet a gentleman of my own class. I dress neat and style, have good clothes and buy what I want. I have been in business for years and have enough means to take care of myself well. American, protestant, high school education, age 59, auburn hair, blue eyes, light complexion, ht. 5-5½, wt. 170, plump figure.

102—Am a widow by death, active and health, live a good, Christian life, plenty of friends, a good cook and housekeeper, a real home lover, believe in cleanliness. American, protestant, grade school education, age 69, grey hair, brown eyes, medium fair complexion, ht. 5-4, wt. 157. Own 40 acre farm and have some money. Would like to hear from a gentleman near my own age.

103—I am quiet and reserved, do not care much for social affairs, love children. No one believes I am as old as I am, and they say I am fine looking. Am experienced in sewing and cooking. American, Methodist, high school education, a clerk, age 46, dark brown hair, brown eyes, good complexion, brunette, ht. 5-3, wt. 150. Own my home. Do not care for riches, just happiness.

104—Am just a plain, everyday woman, neat appearing, considered fairly nice looking, have a cheerful disposition, experienced cook and housekeeper. American - naturalized, Catholic, fair education, age 59, white hair, blue eyes, fair complexion, ht. 5-2, wt. 155. Have $5,000 invested in a home. No objection to a widower by death. I have no desire for wealth.

105—My friends tell me I am very neat appearing, that I dress well and have a good taste for clothing. Am a good cook and housekeeper, like to sew, also like the movies and radio and some travel, and very fond of country life. Albanian, Orthodox religion, fair education, age 48, brown hair and eyes, light complexion, ht. 5 ft., wt. 175. Own two houses.

106—Maiden lady, nice personal appearance, love sports and clean fun, like to go fishing and hunting. Was raised on a farm and like the things you find in country life. American, protestant, grade school education, age 48, light brown hair, light blue eyes, medium fair complexion, ht. 5-2, wt. 118. Own some property. I would not object to a farmer, one of quiet disposition.

107—Am a widow by death, living alone and find life very lonely. I am well respected, truthful and honest, well liked by friends, have a good record in my past life. American, Methodist, common school education, own and operate a store, age 40, brown natural curly hair, blue eyes, fair complexion, ht. 5-3, wt. 110. Worth $3500. Desire companion 40 to 45, truthful and honest.

108—I have a pleasant disposition, have lots of friends, try to enjoy myself any place I go. Lots of people compliment me on my nice appearance, and say I look nice in my clothes. Am a first class cook and housekeeper. American, Baptist, grade school education, a clerk, age 42, black hair, blue eyes, fair complexion, ht. 5-6, wt. 144. Have some means.

109—Am a widow by death, a business woman, living in a small town and being so busy do not have the opportunity to meet men. Am of a kind and affectionate disposition, splendid personality. American, Methodist, good education, age 60, grey hair, blue-grey eyes, fair complexion, ht. 5-8½, wt. 164. Own a home and other means. Desire a companion of good character.

110—Pleasing and sympathetic, like companionship, fond of a quiet life among quiet people, and like to do my own housework. Considered rather nice looking, have a pleasing personality. American, protestant, very good education, age 58, brown greying hair, fair complexion, grey eyes, ht. 5-4, wt. 155. Own a good home, also gas station. Interested in farmer or business man.

111—Am very quiet and affectionate, willing to go out of my way to make anyone happy. Considered very nice appearing, do not dress loud or use makeup. American, Methodist, good education, business woman, age 48, brown hair, blue eyes, light complexion, ht. 5-5, wt. 156. I own and operate a good business, have six employees, also own a nice brick home. Matrimony in view.

112—Considered average in looks, well dressed, can cook and keep house, have some talent in music, can play piano. English, Methodist, fair education, age 37, brown hair, blue eyes, fair complexion, blonde type, ht. 5-2, wt. 100. Have some means. Would like to correspond with a gentleman near my own age, average weight and height, one of fair education.

113—I am rather quiet, home loving, like children. I love music, like to dance some, fond of sports, like to travel, also like the movies. I am graduate of high school, also have three years of college. Am 31 years of age, have blonde hair, brown eyes, ht. 5-8½. Have been employed for past ten years. Have some means. Prefer to hear from business man, one near my age.

114—Am only happy when making someone else happy, and willing to go more than 50-50 with a congenial, good partner. I love outdoor life, a homemaker, a good cook and housekeeper. Am a member of Eastern Star, Rebeccas, Royal Neighbors. American, Baptist, good education, buyer for department store, age 56, light brown greying hair, blue eyes, wt. 150. Some means.

115—I am stout, but very neat appearing and dress nicely. I am a great lover of home, considered a good cook and housekeeper. Am kind and affectionate, have no bad habits, live a quiet life. American, protestant, fair education, age 40, black hair, blue-grey eyes, fair complexion, ht. 5-3, wt. 185. Own a good home. Wish to hear from a nice looking gentleman, good habits.

116—Am a widow by death, kind and good natured. I am rather stout, but not the sloppy kind, as I like to look neat and nice at all times. I own a small poultry ranch of seven acres. American, Baptist, fair education, age 57, brown greying hair, brown eyes, light complexion, ht. 5-6, wt. 185. I have a five room home, also fruit and garden. Desire companion about 60.

118—Am a farmer girl, well experienced cooking and housework, as I help my parents on the farm. Considered rather nice looking, do not dress to extremes, have a good personality, very friendly. Slovak, Lutheran, fair education, age 19, dark blonde hair, grey eyes, medium fair complexion, blonde, ht. 5-3, wt. 140. Wish to hear from young men up to 35 years of age. See my photo above.

117—Honest and ambitious, like to live in pleasant surroundings, do not like people of quarrelsome disposition. Am a widow, considered rather nice looking, pleasant, affectionate disposition, intelligent, nice personality. American, protestant, high school education, age 45, black hair, grey eyes, fair complexion, ht. 5-5, wt. 130. Own small farm. Would marry if suited.

119—Considered rather nice looking, neat appearance, pleasant, lively disposition, well experienced in cooking and keeping house. American, protestant, common school education, age 34, dark hair, brown eyes, fair complexion, brunette type, ht. 5-4, wt. 150. Own home. Would have no objection to a poor man if he proves himself worthy and industrious. Want a good pal and companion.

120—Considered very good looking and neat appearing, also dress nicely. A good cook and housekeeper. Make friends easily, but have few opportunities of meeting new people. American, Methodist, fair education, age 54, light brown hair, blue eyes, fair complexion, ht. 5-4, stout but well proportioned. Own a $6,000 modern home and have some money. Want companion of neat appearance.

121—I am a widow by death, a very good dresser, neat appearing, enjoy good health, no children. I have a good name and stand well where I am known. Was a business woman for many years, know how to meet the public. American, protestant, fair education, middle age, dark brown hair, blue-grey eyes, fair complexion, ht. 5-4, wt. 145. Am in very good financial circumstances.

122—Widow, good, likeable disposition, good character, can give good reference to the right one. Am well liked by business people and friends. American Christian, fair education, age 50, brown and grey hair, fair complexion, grey eyes, ht. 5-8, wt. 145. Am fond of home life, but like some amusement. Own one-half interest in 200 acre farm. Would like to meet a man of good habits.

123—Although well along in years I am considered very active and willing to accept my share of the responsibilities of life. I am a widow by death, neat in appearance, have a pleasing disposition. American, Christion, grammar school education, age 67, light brown hair and eyes, fair complexion, ht. 5-6, wt. 154. Own large home and two tenement houses.

124—I love a nice home and am a good cook and housekeeper. Am not too modern in habits, do not smoke or drink. Am a widow by death, do not have any children, have been left a good home and income. American, protestant, fair education, age 37, dark hair, brown eyes, brunette type, ht. 5-4, wt. 145. Would like to make friends with a view to possible marriage.

125—I stand well in my community and among a host of friends. Am considered neat and attractive, always keep up a good appearance, have a nice personality, look younger than age, also act younger. American, protestant, high school education, age 41, light brown hair and eyes, very good complexion, blonde type, ht. 5-3, wt. 114. Worth about $5,000. Desire companion of good character.

126—Considered rather nice looking and of neat appearance, neatly dressed. A widow by death, no encumbrance, have a good disposition, experienced cook and housekeeper, some talent in music. American, Methodist, two years college education, age 47, blonde hair, blue eyes, fair complexion, ht. 5-2, wt. 139. Have enough means to live comfortably. Want companion older than myself.

127—I am a widow by death, jolly and affectionate disposition, considered nice looking, very neat in appearance, a very good cook and housekeeper. American, protestant, high school education, office worker, age 54, grey hair, hazel eyes, fair complexion, ht. 5-4, wt. 125. Have some means. Money is no object in the one of my choice, but character and truthfulness are essential.

128—Have had plenty of experience in cooking and keeping house, also can do any kind of work on the farm. I have a sunny, rather quiet disposition, enjoy outdoor sports, especially fishing. American, Baptist, fair education, age 39, brown hair and eyes, medium fair complexion, brunette type, ht. 5-6, wt. 124, neat, slender figure. Own a small farm. Would marry if suited. *miss Dora L. wooten RR5 El Dorado ark.*

129—I am a home lover, and can usually be found there. My friends say I am rather nice looking, have a pleasant, jolly disposition, make friends easily, have good business ability, a good cook and housekeeper. Welsh and Irish descent, Baptist, fair education, age 56, grey hair, fair complexion, ht. 5-4, wt. 120. Own a neat, modern home, well furnished. Interested in someone near my own age.

130—I am a widow by death, children all married, and am lonesome for companionship and a happy home. Considered nice looking, refined, a neat dresser, have a lively disposition. Plenty of experience keeping house, an excellent cook. American, protestant, high school education, age 50, brown hair, grey eyes, light complexion, ht. 5-5, wt. 155. Own my home.

131—Refined, neat appearing, have been educated in good schools. When younger have won prizes for my looks and figure. Am a widow by death, do not drink or smoke, have traveled a great deal. American, protestant, well educated, belong to a protestant church, age 45, very dark brown hair, blue eyes, fair complexion, ht. 5-6, wt. 140. Hotel owner and manager.

132—Have always lived on a farm and love farm life. I am a widow, considered rather nice looking and of neat appearance, a hard worker, a good cook and housekeeper. American Christian, fair education, living on farm, age 40, dark brown hair,

brown eyes, fair complexion, brunette, ht. 5-6, wt. 150. Own a farm and stock. Desire a companion that likes farm life, age 38 to 45.

133—I am a church member—ex-school teacher, good disposition, love home, also travel. Am a widow by death, no children, considered to look younger than my age, dress very neatly. American, protestant, well educated, apartment owner and operator, age 50, medium brown hair, blue eyes, fair complexion, ht. 5-1, wt. 135. Worth around $10,000. Wish to correspond for friendship and possibly marriage.

136—I am a rather modest type of person, do not drink or smoke, considered nice looking, neat appearing in my clothes, a good disposition. American, Baptist, common school education, factory worker, age 34; medium brown hair, blue eyes, medium fair complexion. Would like to hear from a nice looking gentleman, not over 40, intelligent, love home. See my photo above. *Bernice Stephenson P.O. Box 158 League City Texas*

134—I am a lonely widow, have a pleasant disposition, dress nicely, well experienced in household duties. I live on a large farm and have 30 head of cows, a two-row tractor and a nice Chevrolet coupe. American, Baptist, high school education, farmerette, age 37, black hair, blue eyes, light complexion, brunette, ht. 5-6, wt. 160. I will be happy to answer all letters that I receive.

mrs Jewell willis RR1.
Stephensville Texas

135—I am loved by all that know me. Have a good disposition, in good health, considered nice looking, a good housekeeper and cook. American, protestant, grade school education, age 45, black hair and eyes, medium fair complexion, ht. 5-4, wt. 148. Own my house and land. Want a companion that could provide for me, with no bad habits, a good worker. Not interested in wealth.

137—Have had special training in hotel work, cooking and sewing. Am easy to get acquainted with, as I have a good personality. Considered neat appearing, have good taste in dress. American, protestant, fair education, age 37, brown hair, grey eyes, fair complexion, brunette type, ht. 5-2, wt. 106. Own small home in country. Desire companion of fair education, decent and respectable.

138—Home loving type, jolly, pleasant disposition, like good clean fun and clean sports. Am rather proud, neat appearance, like to dress well. English-American, Methodist, high school and business course education, age 37, light brown hair, blue eyes, fair complexion, blonde type, ht. 5-6½, wt. 118. Worth $6,000 in property. Not looking for wealth, but a real companion and homemaker.

139—Am not good looking, but considered well dressed and rather attractive. Am a Christian, well respected, a lover of home life. Am a dressmaker and make my own clothes. American, protestant, high school ed-

ucation, age 50, mixed grey hair, grey eyes, fair complexion, ht. 5-7, wt. 165. Own home and car, and have $6,000. Wish to hear from a gentleman 55 to 60, industrious and sober.

140—Very industrious, kind and affectionate disposition, really care for a home, and willing to do my part to make one happy. I am a widow by death, lonely and unhappy. American, protestant, common school education, age 49, dark brown hair, blue eyes, fair complexion, ht. 5-5, wt. 140. Have some means. Would be interested in a man of the home loving type, fair looking and thrifty.

141—I am a widow by death, stand well in my community, have plenty of friends, as I am kind to all I meet. Am rather stout, but a neat dresser and nice looking. American, Christian, common school education, dressmaker, age 64, light brown hair, grey eyes, medium fair complexion, ht. 5-10, wt. 180. Own a five room house, have a nice garden and flock of chickens, also a car.

142—Considered nice looking and of neat appearance, quiet, kind disposition, good character, neither smoke nor drink, experienced cook and housekeeper. American, Methodist, high school education, age 47, black hair, blue-grey eyes, medium fair complexion, brunette type, ht. 5-2, wt. 110. Have some means and will inherit. Interested in a man of good character, age 40 to 65.

143—Have been told that I was good looking, that I carried myself well and that I dressed attractively. Have cheerful, lovable disposition, excellent health, like music, good books, and all sports. American, protestant, college education, school teacher, age 34, brown hair and eyes, fair complexion, brunette, ht. 5-5, wt. 125, neat figure. Own farm, home, and business property.

Jewel Samms
Mc Clure Ill

144—Can furnish reference to the one interested as to character and social standing. Am a widow, have good health, a neat and good dresser. Am very lonely, seeking companionship. American, Presbyterian, common school education, age 53, brown hair, blue eyes, olive complexion, ht. 5-5, wt. 170. Have some means. Desire companion of medium build, nice dresser, weight around 180.

145—Have a fine disposition, well liked by my friends, considered nice looking, a good housekeeper and cook. I am a widow by death, own a 360-acre farm and four room house, and have a good living. American, Christian, common school education, occupation farming, age 31, dark hair, blue eyes, fair complexion, brunette, ht. 5-3, wt. 112. Interested in a good worker, easy to get along with.

146—Am a widow by death, very lonesome, tired of living alone. Would have no objection to a poor man, but want him to come here to live, as I own my home and would not want to dispose of it. French and English descent, Lutheran, grade school education, age 66, dark greying hair, dark eyes, ht. 5-1, wt. 152. Want a companion of affectionate disposition, a Christian preferred.

147—Not considered good looking, but have a good disposition, and I am always nicely dressed and make a neat appearance and look well in my clothes. American, Baptist, fair education, housekeeper, age 51, dark brown hair, blue eyes, fair complexion, ht. 5-7, wt. 140. Have enough means to live well. Wish to hear from a good Christian man, one that likes a good home.

149—Have been a widow for past two years, a business woman, very well educated, a nice personality, dress well, considered nice looking. American, English descent, Methodist, age 48, light brown hair, dark grey eyes, light complexion, ht. 5-4, wt. 160. Own my own home and am self supporting from cafe and hotel business. Desire a companion that is nice looking and well groomed.

148—I am now living with a relative and family, and being lonely would like to make some new friends. I have no special accomplishments, but like to do many things, especially cooking and keeping house. Irish, common school education, age 29, dark brown hair, dark grey eyes, medium fair complexion, ht. 5-8, wt. 140. The one of my choice should be of good character. See my photo above.

150—Considered neat and nice looking, dress in good taste and not too extreme. I am intelligent and industrious, love a nice clean home. American, protestant, common school education, age 50, dark brown hair and eyes, medium fair complexion, ht. 5-1½, wt. 137. Home some means. Am a member of Eastern Star. Want someone well respected, one that would appreciate a nice home and companion.

151—My friends say I am nice looking and a neat dresser. I have a good, congenial education, seamstress, age 60, mixed grey hair, brown eyes, olive complexion, ht. 5-2, wt. 160. Have some money and bonds. Prefer someone in middle class, one with income enough to live in comfort.

152—Have a fine personal appearance, a neat dresser, look well in my clothes, a neat figure, pleasant and jolly disposition, good cook and housekeeper. American, English descent, Baptist, high school education, a nurse, age 50, brown hair and eyes, fair complexion, ht. 5-8, wt. 160. Own a small farm. Would like to hear from a gentleman 60 to 70. Am not seeking riches.

153—I am a lady of good character, considered rather nice looking, a neat dresser, make a very nice appearance, do not have any bad habits, a good cook and housekeeper. American, grade school education, age 56, grey hair, hazel eyes, olive complexion, ht. 5-7, wt. 175. Own house and lot. I have worked hard all of my life, but have no desire for wealth, just want a true companion.

154—Neat, attractive, and well groomed, wear both frilly and tailored clothes. Considered very nice looking, good character, respectable, good cook and housekeeper, can sing and play piano. American, protestant, high school education, office worker, age 40, medium brown hair, blue eyes, fair complexion, ht. 5-2, wt. 135. Own a home. Desire someone jolly and good natured.

155—I would like to correspond with a man that enjoys living on a farm, one of medium height and weight. Would have no objection to a poor man if worthy and industrious. American, fair education, occupation farming, age 39, black hair, brown eyes, light complexion, ht. 5-2, wt. 145. I have 180 acres of land, a good house, some money. Have a good disposition, not bad looking.

156—Considered rather nice looking, and complimented on my neat personal appearance. Can cook and keep house, also do sewing. American, Methodist, college education, age 56, light blonde hair, grey eyes, fair complexion, ht. 5-4½, wt. 150. Own a comfortable home. Would like to correspond with a refined, neat appearing business man. No preference as to kind of business.

157—I have no dependents or encumbrance so can go most any place to live. Was raised on a farm, but in later years have been in business for myself. Considered nice looking, neat appearance, well dressed, a widow by death. German and English descent, common school education, age 52, light brown hair, blue-grey eyes, real fair complexion, ht. 5-3, wt. 140. Have a few thousand dollars.

158—Would prefer to live on a farm or ranch, as I am very fond of country life. People really like me, and I make lots of friends. Considered nice looking and neat appearing. American, Christian, fair education, nurse and housekeeper, age 53, dark brown hair, brown eyes, light complexion, ht. 5-9, wt. 165. Own a home. Want a companion of the home loving type.

159—Widow by death, quiet, sweet disposition, neat dresser, nice appearing, considered young looking for my age. Am home loving, like to cook and keep house, also like a movie once in a while. American, Lutheran, grade school education, practical nurse, age 41, mixed grey hair, light brown eyes, fair complexion, ht. 5-2, wt. 114. Own a home, car and other property.

160—Considered rather nice looking, nice appearing, a neat dresser. Do not drink or smoke, like the movies, cards, dancing, but more fond of home life. American, Catholic, high school education, middle age, curly grey hair, blue eyes, fair complexion, ht. 4-11, wt. 107. Own seven room bungalow, well furnished. Interested in one that is kind, sincere and honest, a real pal.

miss patricia gost RRC.130
Grand Rapids
mich

161—Always neat and well dressed, make a very nice appearance, not too bad looking. Have a cheerful disposition, full of fun, a little on the proud side, careful in making friends. American, Irish descent, fair education, age 42, light brown hair, blue eyes, fair complexion, blonde type, ht. 4-11, wt. 98. Own 40 acre farm, some money. Want someone that likes a nice home and companion.

162—I like to be congenial, have a fine personality, not narrow in my view of any subject. I love to live a simple life, and be a true friend. Considered nice looking, a neat dresser. American, Baptist, good education, operator of grocery, age 35, light brown hair, hazel eyes, fair complexion, ht. 5-10, wt. 135. Have $8,000 cash and property. No objection to a poor man if honest.

163—Widow, have no children, quiet disposition, good looking, neat and dressy appearance, have some talent in music. I owned and operated motion picture theatres for twenty years. American, Episcopalian, two years college education, business woman, age 49, dark brown hair and eyes, fair complexion, ht. 5-6, wt. 147. Have property and cash. Interested in a business man.

164—Widow of two years, lonely, and tired of living alone. Everyone says I am a real nice looking girl, and do not look my age. I am able to look out for myself, but am awful lonesome. American, protestant, fair education, seamstress, age 30, dark brown hair, grey eyes, fair complexion, ht. 5-4, wt. 140. Own my own home with 20 acres. Desire a nice, settled companion of good habits.

165—Have a good reputation, well liked by friends and neighbors, and all that I have known me. Well experienced in household duties, and know how to make a living, but am a widow and very lonely. American, Baptist, common school education, age 58, black and grey hair, blue eyes, fair complexion, ht. 5-5, wt. 175. Own my home. Would like to correspond with a nice gentleman.

166—I am very neat in dress and appearance, and have a nice looking figure, always keep myself looking attractive. Have a kind disposition, rather nice looking, like to dance, can cook and keep house. German and Irish descent, Catholic, high school education, defense worker, age 18, blonde hair, blue eyes, fair complexion, blonde type, ht. 5-9, wt. 145. See my photo above.

167—I am very good company and like good times in the right way. Have been a widow for the past four years, no children. Considered good looking, very neat and good dresser, have a good disposition. American, Catholic, high school education, nurse, age 46, dark hair, blue eyes, fair complexion, brunette, ht. 5-6, wt. 150. Have fair amount of means. Will marry if suited.

168—Am well respected, have a good disposition, dress clean and neat, do not smoke or drink. Am always ready to help anyone in need, and try to make them happy. Irish descent, protestant, common school education, seamstress, age 41, mixed grey hair, hazel eyes, fair complexion, ht. 5-1, wt. 200. Have means. Wish to hear from man of good character, kind disposition, healthy.

169—I am a nurse and all alone at the present time, as my two daughters are married and in homes of their own. Am considered very neat and attractive in appearance. American, protestant, high school and some college education, age 50, black hair, dark brown eyes, olive complexion, ht. 5-5, wt. 170. Own a very nice home. Wish to hear from a middle aged gentleman of neat appearance.

170—Considered fair looking, have a jolly disposition, neat and tidy in my personal appearance, a good cook and neat housekeeper. American, Baptist, common school education, age 59, grey hair, brown eyes, olive complexion, ht. 5-4½, wt. 167. Own my home. Would like to correspond with men that are honest, no bad habits, home loving type, one that can maintain a home.

171—I am a widow by death, have a host of friends. enjoy good times, fond of home life. Considered nice looking, young looking, take pride in keeping up my personal appearance. Am a neat housekeeper and good cook. Play piano for my own amusement. American, Methodist, high school education, age 45, dark brown hair, blue-grey eyes, fair complexion, ht. 5-8, wt. 200. Own home and car.

172—I am a widow, refined, kind, pleasant disposition, nice personal appearance, industrious, like to attend church and social affairs, have some talent in music, a lover of home life. American, English descent, Methodist, high school education, a nurse, age 64, grey hair, hazel eyes, medium fair complexion, ht. 5-3½, wt. 160. Own my home. Gentlemen of suitable age please write.

173—I am a maiden lady, very easy to get along with, experienced housekeeper and cook. Swiss-American, Catholic, fair education, age 48, brown hair and eyes, brunette type, ht. 5-2, wt. 127. I would like to correspond more for amusement for a while until I get letters from men I feel I could care for. I have no desire for wealth. I own a small house and lot.

174—I can do most any kind of work, exceptionally good in cooking and keeping house. I am jolly, and easy to get along with. Irish, Baptist, common school education, age 66, brown hair and eyes, fair complexion, ht. 5-3, wt. 174. Own two houses furnished. Am in the poultry raising business, want someone that would be willing to help me with this line of work.

175—Am a divorcee, considered rather nice looking and very neat in appearance, and of a good disposition. English-American, Methodist, fair education, age 42, chetsnut brown hair, brown eyes, fair complexion, ht. 5-3, wt. 110. Own property valued at $4,500. Wish to hear from one that is honest and sober, fairly intelligent, neat appearing, not bad to look at, age up to 50.

176—My friends consider me nice looking and very attractive. I am industrious, a good, clean housekeeper, taking care of my own home. I have a car and can drive. American, Methodist, good education, age 44, black hair, brown eyes, fair complexion, ht. 5-4, wt. 160. Have some property and money. Desire a companion that is honest and worthy of my confidence.

177—Am of a pleasant disposition refined, a good mixer, have traveled a great deal, excellent taste in clothing, a neat dresser, have no bad habits. American, protestant, well educated, age 52, light brown hair, brown eyes, fair complexion, ht. 5-2, wt. 108. Have my own home and income. Worth $6,000. I do not care for the loud, rough type of person. Want a good, honest companion.

178—Considered very good looking, and young looking for my age. Neat and attractive, always dressed well enough to look nice. I am a quiet type of person, love home life, take a great interest in keeping house. American, Baptist, common school education, age 39, brown hair, blue eyes, fair complexion, ht. 5-6, wt. 130. Own my home. Interested in a home lover, 39 to 49.

179—Well experienced in keeping house and cooking, also in nursing. Considered young looking for age, have no grey hair, a good dresser, in good health. American, Methodist, high school education, defense worker at present time, age 54, brown hair, blue eyes, clear, fair complexion, ht. 5-9, wt. 167. Some means. Want someone that cares more for a companion than wealth.

180—Widow by death, jolly disposition, even temperament, do not drink or smoke, in good health. American, Baptist, teacher, normal school education, age 38, dark brown hair, blue eyes, light complexion, ht. 5-8½, wt. 180. Worth $2,000, income $1,000 yearly. Would like someone with a good disposition, near my own age, who likes all kinds of sports and music, with fair income.

181—Considered fairly nice looking, neat and attractive, good natured disposition, well thought of by all my neighbors, friends and employer. American, protestant, common school education, age 54, brown hair, hazel eyes, medium fair complexion, ht. 5-3½, wt. 150. Worth $3200. Would like to correspond with a gentleman that is good natured and easy to get along with.

182—Am a widow by death, kind, honest and true. I can do most any kind of housework and cooking, in best of health. American, common school education, age 42, dark brown greying hair, blue-grey eyes, fair complexion, ht. 5-7, wt. 150. I own my own home and a small farm. Would like to meet a gentleman near my own age, one that does not drink, and is honest and kind.

183—American, protestant, fair education, a nurse, age 50, medium brown hair, blue-grey eyes, fair complexion, ht. 5 ft., wt. 160. Am a widow, one son married. Am considered fair looking and of neat appearance. Have some means. Would like to hear from someone in the fifties, good habits, and enjoys good, clean sports. Would have no objection to a poor man if worthy.

184—People say that I have a nice appearance, and they also like my company. Am considered good looking, have a nice disposition, can cook and keep house. American, Baptist, high school education, age 19, dark hair, brown eyes, medium fair complexion, brunette type, ht. 5-10, wt. 165. Wish to hear from a young man that is nice looking. See my photo above.

185—Very attractive, good housekeeper and cook, and very neat about my personal appearance, always well dressed. I like cards, radio, movies, and company in my own home. American, German descent, protestant, fair education, age 49, dark brown hair and eyes, olive complexion, ht. 5-5, wt. 185. Own my home. Desire someone who can appreciate a good home.

186—I am a widow by death, a dependable person, a home lover, kind and affectionate disposition, a good cook and housekeeper. Have been in business for myself, but retired now. American, Lutheran, good education, age 52, brown hair, blue eyes, light complexion, ht. 5-2, wt. 151. Worth $8,000. Have been a widow for three years, very lonely. Wish to hear from one near my own age.

187—I love home life, all clean sports, shows, a nice home and surroundings. I am very economical, do not drink or smoke, young looking for age, a stylish, smart dresser, outstanding for amount I spend on clothes. American, Methodist, high school education, age 52, brown and grey hair, blue eyes, medium fair complexion, ht. 5-3, wt. 115. $2,000 in property, also cash and bonds.

188—I was raised on farms and ranches, know how to get the most out of a dollar. Am kind and very affectionate, nice looking, a good cook and neat housekeeper. Irish and English descent, grade school education, age 45, reddish brown hair, blue eyes, fair complexion, ht. 5-2, wt. 125. Worth $5,000. No objection to a poor man if he were a nice, congenial person.

189—I am a widow, have no dependents, a good business woman, own my own business, have a nice income from same. I am considered intelligent, nice looking, a neat dresser. American, Baptist, fair education, age 60, brown hair, blue eyes, fair complexion, ht. 5-5, wt. 156. Worth $5,000. Wish to hear from a gentleman over 60, nice looking, a neat dresser, kind and affectionate.

190—I am a good housekeeper, fond of home, refined, quiet disposition. Widow by death, no children or dependents, neat and attractive in appearance. American, protestant, common school education, a clerk, age 60, brown and grey hair, blue eyes, fair complexion, ht. 5-5, wt. 125. Have some means. Interested in a gentleman not over 65, kind disposition, fond of home life.

191—Considered very good looking, neat and attractive appearance, make all my own clothes. I am living alone and very lonely for companionship. French, common school education, age 38, black hair and eyes, olive complexion, brunette type, ht. 5-1½, wt. 125, neat figure. I own my home and furniture. Desire a companion that could come here to live. Prefer a poor, working man.

192—I enjoy dancing, riding, fishing, in fact I cannot really say there is a sport I do not enjoy. I am neat at all times, and very well mannered. Irish-French, Methodist, well educated, age 21, chestnut auburn hair, brown eyes, fair complexion, ht. 5-7½, wt. 118, nice figure. Wish to hear from a young man nicely built, neat appearing, clean cut. See my photo above.

193—Have a jolly disposition and a good sense of humor. Have been cooking and keeping house practically all of my life. Am industrious, considered neat appearing. American, Christian, common school education, age 57, dark brown hair, blue eyes, light complexion, ht. 4-11, wt. 124. Own a home. Desire a companion serious minded, intelligent, religiously inclined.

194—Am a widow by divorce, considered nice looking, neat and attractive in dressing. Am very fond of home life, a good cook and housekeeper, like to take care of my own home. Irish-American, grade school education, age 45, brown hair, olive complexion, brunette type, ht. 5-5, wt. 175. Own home and car. Would like to hear from a railroad man, but will consider others.

195—I have natural, charming manners, although somewhat reserved or timid in some situations, but create a good impression on all I meet. I have good judgment and understand the importance of economy. American, Lutheran, college education, age 48, blonde and grey hair, fair complexion, grey eyes, ht. 5-6, wt. 128. Own a small farm. Desire an honest, loyal companion.

196—Have always been highly respected, but am jolly and good natured and like fun out of life. Am always well groomed and have good taste for attractive and suitable clothing. American, Baptist, fair education, age 49, brown hair, blue eyes, fair complexion, ht. 5-7, wt. 115. Occupation stock farming. Would like to hear from a good looking, well mannered man, nice personality.

197—Considered nice looking, neat in appearance, a good disposition, good housekeeper and cook. Have some talent in music, play violin. American, Christian, common school education, age 55, brown hair, blue eyes, fair complexion, brunette, ht. 5-4, wt. 148. Some means. Am not seeking a wealthy companion, but one that could make me a good living.

198—I am a good housekeeper and excellent cook. I have traveled some, read a lot, and people always say they enjoy my company, as I am not tiresome, do not talk foolishness. American, Methodist, fair education, age 52, dark brown greying hair, hazel eyes, good complexion, ht. 5-8, wt. 165. Own my home. Interested in someone nice looking, a good worker.

199—Have a good personality, considered fair looking, kind disposition, friendly attitude toward everyone. Am well experienced in cooking and keeping house. American, Christian, common school education, a nurse, age 55, brown greying hair, blue eyes, olive complexion, ht. 5-4, wt. 145. Own a home and stock. Would have no objection to a poor man if worthy and honest.

200—Considered very neat and attractive in appearance, have a sunny disposition, experienced in cooking and keeping house. American, protestant, college education, school teacher, age 40, black hair, dark brown eyes, medium fair complexion, brunette type, ht. 5-6, wt. 140. Own real estate and personal property. Wish to hear from men of good character.

201—I like farm life very much, and would want a companion that is willing to work and want to make a good home. I am fond of kind, good, generous people. German and Irish descent, Methodist, common school education, age 56, brown hair, blue eyes, light complexion, ht. 5-3, wt. 170. Own 50 acre farm. Would like someone interested in farm life.

202—I am considered not bad looking, always neat and attractively dressed, like things clean around my home. American, protestant, grade school education, age 55, light brown hair, blue eyes, fair complexion, ht. 5-7, wt. 135. Have $2,000. Wish to correspond with a gentleman near my own age, one that is kind, wants a good home and companionship.

Birdie L. Horsington RR. 5
Shawnee Okla.

203—I have a good disposition, and am easy to get along with. Have had plenty of experience in cooking and keeping house. Considered rather nice looking. American, protestant, common school education, age 39, brown greying hair, blue-grey eyes, fair complexion, ht. 5-7, wt. 215. Own farming outfit. Wish to hear from farmer or rancher, one who is fair looking.

204—Widow by death, a Christian, a member of Eastern Star and White Shrine, nice appearing, a good disposition, good cook and housekeeper, no dependent or encumbrance. American, Baptist, high school education, matron of dormitory, age 52, light brown hair, hazel eyes, fair complexion, ht. 5-5, wt. 150. Own a modern home. Desire a Christian companion.

205—I am a good, faithful type of person, kind and true, pleasant disposition, well liked by all who know me. I am a good housekeeper and cook, and a willing worker. American, Methodist, fair education, age 60, dark brown hair, grey eyes, fair complexion, ht. 5-7, wt. 180. Own a ten room rooming house, well furnished. Am a furrier and make good money fall and winter.

206—Am a widow, no children, considered nice looking, very neat in dress, good taste in clothing, a clean, good housekeeper and cook, like any nice entertainment. American, grade school education, age 45, grey hair, dark brown eyes, fair complexion, ht. 5-2, wt. 120. Worth $3,000. Want a companion that is truthful and honest, willing to help make a home and happiness.

207—A pleasing personality, good disposition, enjoy fishing, picnicking, company, do not dance. I have business experience and get along very well in dealing with the public. American, Baptist, two years high school education, clerk and cashier, age 45, brown greying hair, blue eyes, fair complexion, ht. 5-3, wt. 110. Own three pieces of property.

208—I am smart appearing, honest, well liked and trusted by my business associates. Considered nice looking, and have a fine personality. American, Protestant, high school education, age 39, brown hair, blue eyes, medium fair, ht. 5-6, wt. 135. Own two farms. I have these farms and must stay here and keep my home. I have quite a place here, and need honest co-operation.

211—I am of a jolly, pleasant nature, like outdoor sports, fond of dancing, but can do without it. Considered very attractive and neat, wear my clothes well. French descent, Catholic, high school and some college education, saleslady, age 33, black hair, dark brown eyes, olive complexion, brunette, ht. 5-4, wt. 134. Interested in someone with fair education. See my photo above.

209—I am a widow by death, have a good education, play piano some, a good cook and housekeeper, considered rather nice looking for age. I like to visit and go to nice places. I own a good six room house, a nice home. Scotch-Irish, Baptist, age 68, grey hair, blue-grey eyes, fair complexion, ht. 5-7, wt. 170. Wish to hear from a man of good habits, home loving.

210—I am easy to get along with, as I have a good disposition. Would be glad to find someone that likes farm life, as I am fond of the country and like to raise chickens and do a lot of other work. American, Christian, fair education, age 55, brown hair and eyes, fair complexion, ht. 5-2, wt. 145. Own two good homes. Am alone and would be willing to marry a poor man if honest.

212—I am not the drinking type, but I do like my cigarettes. I enjoy keeping a neat house, also like to keep myself neat. Considered very nice looking, have a good natured disposition. English and Syrian, Catholic, high school education, have some talent in music, age 43, black hair, brown eyes, olive complexion, brunette type, ht. 5-2, wt. 140. Own a home.

213—I have a good disposition, and splendid personality, fond of a quiet home life, make friends easily if they are my type. American, Protestant, college education, seamstress, age 39, dark brown hair, grey eyes, olive complexion, brunette type, ht. 5-5, wt. 130. Worth $2,000. Would like to hear from bachelor or widower by death. Will exchange photos.

214—Am an active woman, carry on my home, drive my car, and attend to all financial matters. I have a nice home and quite a lot of property and situated nicely financially, but the home is not complete without someone to share it. American, protestant, fair education, play piano, age 65, grey hair, good complexion, grey eyes, ht. 5 ft., wt. 120. Worth $6,000 in money and property.

215—I am very attractive and good looking, of good moral character, intelligent, have a great interest in church work. I have a pleasing personality and can meet the public. American, Baptist, high school and business college graduate, stenographer, age 23, auburn hair, blue-grey eyes, fair complexion, wt. 120. Financial worth, $4,000. Interested in a sincere, reliable type of person.

216—I do not smoke or drink or have any bad habits. I am a good cook and housekeeper, fond of the out-of-doors, and like to go on camping trips. Considered good looking, look nice in my clothes. American, Methodist, two years high school education, age 45, brown hair and eyes, fair complexion, ht. 5-4, wt. 128, very nice figure. Own a nice home. Matrimony in view.

217—Considered very good looking for age, and have many compliments on my neat appearance and taste in dressing. I have a pleasant personality, kind hearted, love to cook and keep a neat, clean house. American, Catholic, grade school education, age 50, partly grey hair, blue eyes, fair complexion, ht. 5-3½, wt. 145. Some means. Desire a companion of good character.

218 — Widow by death, very nice looking, have a neat figure and wear my clothes well and in good taste, have poise. I like to go places, but I also like to stay home with congenial company. American, Protestant, college education, age 58, dark brown greying hair, blue eyes, very fair complexion, ht. 5-4, wt. 142. Own property worth about $10,000. Will marry if suited.

219—Am a widow by death, in good health, no encumbrance, very neat, smart and intelligent looking. American, Baptist, age 44, brown hair, blue eyes, fair complexion, ht. 5-5, wt. 160. Have means. Have sufficient means to retire, but am lonely and would enjoy corresponding with a gentleman of good standing, who is like myself lonely, and would appreciate a sincere companion.

220—Nurse, nice looking, well educated, good dresser, kind disposition, good personality. American, Methodist, high school, business college and nurses training education, age 48, dark brown hair, blue eyes, fair complexion, ht. 5-6, wt. 140. Worth $5,000. Wish to correspond with a gentleman who is well educated and would appreciate the friendship of a lady of refinement.

221—Am occupied in keeping apartment house, have good health, like to go out for a good time occasionally, and like to have company. Not considered good looking, but have a nice appearance. American, common school education, age 63, brown hair, grey eyes, fair complexion, ht. 5ft., wt. 155. Worth $4,000. Wish to hear from one that likes to enjoy life in a nice way.

222—Am a widow by death, kind and affectionate, always neatly dressed, intelligent looking, have talent in music. American, protestant, grammar school education, age 44, black hair, blue eyes, fair complexion, brunette, ht. 5-5, wt. 138. Own a farm. Would like to hear from a widower by death, or bachelor, good character, and near my age if possible.

223—A lady of very refined habits, no smoking or drinking, but like good, clean entertainment and best of social activities. Very neat appearance, well dressed, winning personality. American, Episcopalian, high school education, retire, age 52, grey hair, fair complexion, grey eyes, ht. 5-2, wt. 145. Own home worth $3,500, small bank account. Matrimonial intentions.

224—Sunny and cheerful disposition, nice looking, very attractive in dress and appearance, some talent in music, business experience. American, protestant, high school education, age 58, dark brown greying hair, grey eyes, good complexion, ht. 5-2, wt. 137. Some means. Wish to hear from a clean, upright man, with good looks, good dresser, a good business man.

225—A hard worker myself, but not a slave driver. Own a 20-acre farm, poultry, etc. Have made my living with poultry, could make good with help. Considered neat appearing and fairly good looking for age. American, protestant, grade school education, age 65, grey hair, blue eyes, fair complexion, ht. 5-5, wt. 160. Wish to hear from one willing to co-operate.

226—I am able to support myself, so do not need a companion to support me, but do get lonely. My friends say I look much younger than my age, that I am attractive and a neat dresser. American, Baptist, common school education, age 65, brown hair and eyes, fair complexion, ht. 5-6, wt. 165. Own a nice farm in Illinois. The one of my choice must be of good habits.

227—Neat and trim in appearance, nice looking, and I try to live up to the mark. American, protestant, high school and business training education, age 54, medium brown hair, blue-grey eyes, fair complexion, ht. 5-4, wt. 145. Own some real estate. Would like to meet a gentleman around my own age, who would like a sincere pal and helpmate.

228—Am considered neat and tidy in appearance, and have a pleasant personality, congenial disposition, nice looking, considered excellent cook and homemaker. American, high school education, age 38, dark brown hair and eyes, olive complexion, brunette type, ht. 5-3, wt 185. Own home. Will consider matrimony if suited. The one of my choice need not be rich.

229—Have no special talent or accomplishments, only experienced in household duties. Widow by death, considered good looking, retired from a life on the farm. American, Methodist, common school education, age 60, light brown hair, brown eyes, fair complexion, ht. 5ft., wt. 145. Own 160-acre farm. Wish a true, affectionate companion, some means.

230—Considered nice looking, natural wavy hair, very good taste in choosing my clothing. Am a very good cook and housekeeper. American, high school education, age 26. auburn hair, grey eyes, fair complexion, ht. 5-2, wt. 134. Have a gay, cheerful disposition. Am very lonely and would like to receive letters from gentlemen 28 to 45. See my photo above.

231—Widow by death, very affectionate, good, honest, kind, sincere, home loving, respected, considered very attractive and good looking. American, Baptist, grammar school education, age 48, black hair, hazel eyes, fair complexion, ht. 5-2, wt. 150. Own home valued at $3,500, and will inherit farm. Desire companion home loving, of good standing.

232—Am very lonely on a big farm in Iowa, after losing my husband. I love to drive a car, and go out occasionally for a good time, also like to go to Church. Neat appearing, good looking, dress nice. American, Catholic, grade school education, age 38, brown hair and eyes, fair complexion, brunette, ht. 5-4, wt. 125. Would like a real home loving companion.

233—Clean both morally and personally, sincere, honest and upright, held in high esteem, can appreciate the better things of life. Good figure, dress becomingly, attractive in appearance. American, protestant, high school education, Supervisor Dietetics, age 53, brown hair and eyes, medium fair complexion, ht. 5-4, wt. 145. Have some means.

234—American, good, kind disposition, good housekeeper and cook, tolerant of all religions, age 57, blonde hair turning grey, blue eyes, fair complexion, ht. 5-4. wt. 145, common school education. Own a good farm, good house well furnished with everything needed. Want a good, kind companion, that does not drink or gamble. willing to come here to live.

235—Prefer men of the medium class, a willing worker, must love the country. I live on my 80-acre farm, have stock poultry. Protestant, jolly, cheerful disposition, age 54, brown hair and eyes, ht. 5-2, average weight 120. I like music, most any kind of fancy work, and love my home. No one who uses liquor need write to me.

236—I am a widow by death for past six years, and very lonely for a good companion. People say I am nice looking for my age. I like to dress good and look nice. American, common school education, protestant, age 56, blonde hair, grey eyes, ht. 5-2½, wt. 175. Own house and lot and household furniture. Would marry if suited, one with a means of support.

237—I have been in business for myself, know how to meet the public. A good cook and housekeeper, do not smoke or drink, believe in doing right, like to go to church. Fairly good looking, neat appearance. American, college education, nurse, age 57, brown hair, blue eyes, fair complexion, ht. 5-5, wt. 128. Own a home. Ranchers or business men please write.

238—Considered rather nice looking, have a cheerful disposition, neat in appearance, love my home. American, protestant, high school education, age 34, dark brown hair, blue eyes, fair complexion, brunette type, ht. 5-5, wt. 130. Own my home. Would consider matrimony if suited. Wish to correspond with a home loving gentleman, no bad habits.

239—Am occupied in farming, have some talent in music, a good housekeeper and cook, considered nice looking, neat appearance, have a kind disposition. French and Irish descent, protestant, high school education, age 47, dark hair, hazel eyes, light complexion, brunette, ht. 5-4, wt. 139, very neat figure. I own property. Desire a good, sober companion, no children.

240—Widow by death for past tour years, good reputation, do not smoke, drink or play cards, no encumbrance, alone, considered nice looking, neat in dress and appearance. American, Baptist, high school education, age 48, brown hair and eyes, fair complexion, ht. 5-2, wt. 175. Own a home and some vacant property. My desire is a true, Christian companion.

241—Am not interested in riches, as character counts with me. I am very energetic, love my home, a steady worker, no bad habits, considered good looking, very neat in appearance. American, English descent, Methodist, high school education, age 39, dark brown hair, deep blue eyes, fair complexion, ht. 5-7, wt. 145. Own my home and household goods.

242—My friends say I always look nice, have nice clothes, a good housekeeper and cook. American, fair education, age 48, brown hair, fair complexion, brunette type, slender, wt. 132, good figure. Own my home. Would like to correspond with a nice looking gentleman, weighing about 190, well dressed, ambitious, no farmer, as I prefer to live in the city.

243—Young for years, home loving, good health, a widow by death, nice looking, easy to get along with, neat in dress. Good disposition. American, French and Irish descent, Methodist, two years college education, age 53, grey hair, light complexion, grey eyes, ht. 5-1, wt. 107. Some means. Wish to hear from home loving type, good morals, kind and true.

244—Am a widow by death, honest, do not drink or smoke, affectionate, friendly disposition, always neat appearing, have lots of nice friends. Own my home, rent apartments for income. American, Baptist, common school education, age 51, grey hair, blue eyes, fair complexion, ht. 5-4, wt. 160. Desire a companion of good habits, respectable and honest.

245—American, protestant faith, fair education, age 44, brown hair, blue eyes, fair complexion, ht. 5-3, wt. 131. Home owner, single by divorce. Work as an assembler in the Ford plant. Would like to correspond with a gentleman between the ages of 40 and 55, one who loves home life and the better things of life. Matrimony in view if suited.

246—Good natured, sensible, lover of home life, do not enjoy running around. Am well liked by all who know me. Am a widow by death, and am very lonely. American, Methodist, common school education, age 65, brown hair, blue eyes, fair complexion, ht. 5-4, wt. 125. Own my home in the country. No objection to a poor man if industrious, and is kind and affectionate.

247—Am just a farmer lady, but everyone says I look neat and tidy, look well in my clothes. I am a good entertainer, have lots of friends, like all kinds of sports, a good cook. American, grade school education, age 39, black hair, brown eyes, fair complexion, ht. 5-6, wt. 120. Own farm. Wish to hear from one fairly good looking, age 50 to 55.

251—Am considered pretty, neat appearing, like simple, but nice clothes. Am ambitious, love fun and gayety, like writing and receiving letters, some talent in writing and fashion designing. American, Czech descent, Methodist, high school education, clerk, age 22, blonde hair, blue eyes, fair complexion, ht. 5-5, wt. 113. Wish to hear from young men 22 to 30. See my photo above.

248—I like friends, family, home, lover of nature, like music and dancing. I have done lots of social service work, besides raising and providing for my family. American, English descent, elementary school and business education, some talent in music, age 51, brown and grey hair, brown eyes, medium fair complexion, ht. 5-3, wt. 140, neat figure. Own property.

249—I have a good disposition, not so hard to get along with, have good health, dress neat, make a nice appearance, love the care of a nice home, music and amusements. American, Christian, grade school education, age 67, grey hair, brown eyes, fair complexion, ht. 5-5, wt. 140. Own a

modern home. Will do my part in maintaining a home for the right one.

250—Am considered attractive and well dressed, have a pleasing personality, a very good cook and housekeeper. American, French and Irish descent, Catholic, high school education, office worker, age 35, blonde hair, blue eyes, fair complexion, blonde type, ht. 5-6, wt. 135, good figure. Would like to hear from a clean cut gentleman over 40 years of age.

252—Considered above the average in appearance, nice looking, very capable, honest, respectable, can mix with any class of people, good conversationalist, young looking. American, protestant, part college education, age 63, black hair, brown eyes, medium fair complexion, ht. 5-6, wt 160. Have money and bonds. Desire average looking companion, intelligent, capable.

253—I am somewhat on the old fashioned type, a neat, plain dresser, not much for fussy apparel, but dress in good taste. Have congenial, sunny disposition, love the outdoors, nice looking. American, protestant, two years college education, secretary, age 48, brown greying hair, brown eyes, fair complexion, ht. 5-7½, wt. 180. Worth $15,000, will inherit $20,000.

254—My younger days were spent in an office, therefore like the business class of people. Have a good disposition, considered nice looking, neat appearing, some talent in music. American, Catholic, high school and some college education, manager of apartment house, age 54, brown hair and eyes, medium fair complexion, ht. 5-6½, wt. 150. In good circumstances.

255—Friends say I am nice looking for one of my age. Am a widow alone, refined, neat appearing, in comfortable circumstances, some cash and personal property, a small income. American, Baptist, high school education, age 53, mixed grey hair, black eyes, olive complexion, ht. 5-5, wt. 143. Wish to hear from one of good habits, a Christian, loves home life.

256—I am living on a farm, know how to do all kinds of farm work, a good cook and clean housekeeper. Considered intelligent, have a mild disposition, fair looking. American, protestant, common school education, age 52, brown hair, grey eyes, fair complexion, ht. 5-3, wt. 140. Own home, will inherit farm. Wish to hear from a gentleman 50 to 60 years of age.

257—Have a good and kind disposition, and everybody I meet likes my appearance. Am easy to get along with and am well liked by my friends. American, protestant, grade school education, occupation farming, age 38, brown hair, blue eyes, fair complexion, ht. 5-3, wt. 192. Some means. Would have no objection to a poor man if of good disposition, and a good manager.

258—Considered nice looking, young in appearance, industrious, home loving, have a good disposition and easy to get along with, and above all a good cook and housekeeper. American, Methodist, common school education, age 58, light brown hair, blue eyes, fair complexion, ht. 4-9, wt. 125. Own my home, and want a companion that would be willing to live in my home.

259—Am healthy, red rosy cheeks, do not have to use make up. Am considered good looking by my friends, and have a good disposition, a good cook and housekeeper. American, Baptist, common school education, seamstress, age 46, brown hair, blue eyes, fair complexion, blonde, ht. 5-2, wt. 171. Own home and one-acre of ground in small town. Would like to hear from a farmer.

260—Like to dance, play cards, outdoor life, can sew, good cook, economical, industrious, jolly and good natured, mix well, can keep friends, do not keep bad company, no bad habits. Norwegian, protestant, fair education, age 44, brown hair, blue eyes, fair complexion, brunette, ht. 5-2, wt. 165. Own my home. Wish to hear from the working type, no drinker.

261—I am of protestant faith, believe in the golden rule, have a very kind disposition, nice looking, make a good appearance. American, protestant, high school education, age 48, brown hair, blue eyes, fair complexion, ht. 5-3, wt. 138, good figure. Some means. I like a good, Christian character, one who could furnish a home, or go 50-50.

262—I am a woman of means, no dependents, educated and refined, from a good family background, pretty and attractive, stylish dresser, widowed by death, retired. American, Methodist, graduate of girls school, age 45, auburn hair, grey-blue eyes, fair complexion, ht. 5-3, wt. 108. Own new bungalow and some acreage. The one of my choice must be of good character, good disposition.

263—I have been told lots of times that I was a good woman and a fine neighbor. I have a good disposition, nice looking, very neat in appearance, have some talent in music. American, Baptist, fair education, age 47, dark brown hair, grey eyes, fair complexion, ht. 5-2, wt. 161. Own my home. Wish to hear from one that is neat and clean, no drinking man.

264—Considered very nice looking, appearing much younger, full of life, I work hard and play just as hard, really enjoy friends and entertaining, can adjust myself to any environment. American, protestant, one year college education, office worker, age 42, light brown hair, grey eyes, fair complexion, ht. 5-5, wt. 148. Make good salary and have comfortable home.

265—Have had many compliments, quite attractive for one of my age. Am good natured, love clean fun, have traveled a great deal, but am alone now after many years of home life, and find it very lonely. American, protestant, common school education, age 57, brown and grey hair, blue-grey eyes, ht. 5-7, wt. 160. Own my home and have Annuity Policy from which I live.

266—Receive many compliments on my personal appearance, as I always try to dress neat and attractive. I have a kind, jolly, friendly disposition, do not smoke or drink, have a good reputation. American, Slovak descent, Catholic, fair education, age 18, dark hair, dark brown eyes, olive complexion, ht. 5-4, wt. 115. Wish to hear from young men of good habits. See my photo above.

267—Live a quiet life, keep the best of company, have never used tobacco in any form, considered very neat and attractive in appearance, have a good disposition. English, Christian Scientist, high school and college education, occupied in home duties, age 48, dark brown hair, dark blue eyes, medium fair complexion, ht. 5-5, wt. 125. Some means.

268—Passingly good looking, rather stout, but good figure, have a good disposition. Have many years of experience in cooking and keeping house. I own 70 acres of land, some money in bank and three houses. American, Methodist, common school education, retired, age 63, gray hair, light complexion, grey eyes, ht. 5-7, wt. 175.

Wish to hear from nice appearing gentleman.

269—Am considered very neat and attractive, have a good, kind disposition, stand well in my community, a lover of home life. French and Irish descent, protestant, high school education, age 52, brown greying hair, brown eyes, fair complexion, ht. 5-7, wt. 170. Own some land. Would like to hear from a gentleman near my age, good character, honest and true.

270—Would like to correspond with a gentleman 25 to 36 years of age, one who likes to work on a farm. I am a widow, considered rather nice looking, dress well but not expensively, easy to get along with. American, Christian, common school education, age 22, blonde hair, blue eyes, fair complexion, blonde type, ht. 5 ft., wt. 114. Own a farm and equipment.

271—American, Baptist, fair education, have a pleasing disposition, well experienced in all household duties. Brunette type, age 37, dark hair, grey eyes, olive complexion, ht. 4-11, wt. 116, nice appearance, well dressed. Own my home. I would like to correspond with a middle age gentleman, dark type. No objection to a poor man if he proves himself worthy and industrious.

272—Pleasing personality, congenial, attractive, neat appearance, dress in good taste, intelligent, good conversationalist, make friends without much effort. American, college education, business lady, age 52, brown greying hair, hazel eyes, fair complexion, ht. 5-5, wt. 175. Own a residence, farm and business. Would like to hear from one that has had a reasonable amount of success.

273—Am a farmerette, also taught school. Do not care for society, but would love a home with not too much responsibility. I am not beautiful, but look nice in my clothes and am attractive. American, Baptist, one year in college, age 52, dark brown hair, hazel eyes, fair complexion, ht. 5-3, wt. 112. Own 90 acres of land and some money. Am a maiden lady.

274—I am a widow and very lonely, and would like very much to meet my ideal soon, as I am tired of living alone. Considered rather nice looking, dress well, young looking. American, Baptist, common school education, age 36, dark brown hair, dark blue eyes, medium fair complexion, ht. 5-4, wt. 120, neat figure. I own 40 acre farm.

275—I have a pleasing disposition, loved and respected by all who know me. Am neat and nice appearing at all times, a good cook and housekeeper. American, Baptist, common school education, age 58, brown hair mixed with grey, brown eyes, olive complexion, ht. 5-4, wt. 103. I have a nice home. Would prefer to hear from a railroad man, but would consider others.

276—Have been a farmer's wife, have been a hard working woman all my life, but have retired and live in town now. American, Methodist, common school education, age 65, brown and grey hair, brown eyes, medium fair complexion, ht. 5-3, wt. 140. Worth $10,000. Prefer a companion that is industrious, good habits, clean and honest, not destitute.

277—I have a kind disposition, affectionate, no bad habits, a lover of home, like flowers, music, art, movies, traveling. Am rather distinguished looking, look well in my clothes. English, Methodist, common school education, age 50, dark hair, brown eyes, olive complexion, ht. 5-6, wt. 160. Own a home and some money. Wish to hear from a Christian gentleman.

278—Am a widow by divorce, no children, fair looking, neat appearing, a good cook and housekeeper, like home work, but work in defense work at present time. English and Irish descent, protestant, common school education, age 51, brown hair and eyes, fair complexion, ht. 5-6, wt. 148. Own my home. Would like to hear from a farmer, sober, good worker, honest.

279—I am a widow by death, of neat appearance and a good dresser, well experienced in cooking and keeping house, a neat dresser, nice appearance. American, Christian, fair education, age 60, black hair slightly grey, brown eyes, ht. 5-7, wt. 135. Own my home and a farm. Would like to hear from a good man that is lonely like myself. Have no desire for a rich man.

280—People say I am friendly, honest, and easy to get along with. Considered fairly nice looking, pleasing disposition, neat appearing. American, Methodist, fair education, age 50, brown hair, blue eyes, light complexion, ht. 5-5, wt. 140. Have some means. Would like to correspond with most any nice gentleman around 50 years of age.

284—My friends tell me I have beautiful, bright eyes, that I dress very nice, and know how to dress my hair. I have some talent in music—play the Spanish guitar. French, Catholic, two years high school education, store clerk, age 20, black hair and eyes, fair complexion, brunette type, ht. 5-2, wt. 115. Prefer someone who likes music and sports, age 20 to 24. See my photo above.

281—Widow by death, practical nurse, sympathetic, kind disposition, good health, love to work, experienced housekeeper and cook, considered nice looking and rather attractive. American, Irish descent, Baptist, common school education, age 45, dark brown hair, blue eyes, fair complexion, ht. 5-2, wt. 110. Own a home. Desire a companion of good habits, likes quiet home life.

282—I would not care for a rich man, as I have a good living for two, if only I had someone to help me. Am considered good looking for a lady of my age, and make a nice appearance. American, Baptist, common school education, age 50, dark brown hair, blue eyes, fair complexion, ht. 5-2, wt. 135. Own a 90 acre farm, stock and car. Wish to hear from one near my age.

283—My friends say I am neat appearing and nice looking for my age. Am a very timid person, but kind and affectionate. All alone and very lonely. American, golden rule religion, common school and business education, age 53, brown hair, blue eyes, fair complexion, ht 5-4, wt. 115. Own 110 acre farm with five room modern house. Wish to hear from someone near my age.

285—Have a sunny disposition, like to mingle with people, neat appearing, carry myself well, considered good looking, a neat dresser, industrious around home, very good cook and housekeeper. Polish-American, Catholic, age 32, blonde hair, hazel eyes, fair complexion, ht. 5-1, wt. 122, nice, shapely figure. Own real estate and other property. Matrimony in view.

286—Am considered a very attractive woman, with a very pleasing personality, and wear my clothes well. Very affectionate disposition, accomplished in music, play piano. American, Irish descent, college education, age 48, grey hair, worth $5000. Wish to hear from a tall, clean cut gentleman, one who has a sense of humor.

287—I have an excellent character, do not smoke or drink, or go to any places of questionable amusement. Am considered neat and attractive in personal appearance and young looking. American, protestant, common school education, some musical talent, age 37, brown hair, blue eyes, fair complexion, brunette type, ht. 5-5, wt. 140. Own home. Wish to hear from farmers or ranchers.

288—Cheerful, friendly, good natured disposition, nice looking and refined, sincere, capable; making my own living, healthy and active, like good music, literature. English-American, Presbyterian, graduate nurse, age 54, blonde and grey hair, hazel eyes, fair complexion, ht. 5-3, wt. 120. Own home and acreage. Wish to hear from one who is kind and genteel.

289—Widow by death, very good disposition, neat in appearance, do not smoke or use profane language, and have a good personality. American, protestant, common school education, age 51, dark brown hair, brown eyes, medium fair complexion, ht. 5-6, wt. 198. Own my home. I would work as best I could to help a poor man along if he were honest and industrious.

290—I have beautiful hair, attractive features, sparkling eyes, a nice personality. I love to read, keep house, dress nice, enjoy good music, good singer, like to work out of doors. Dutch, Lutheran, good education, age 36, dark brown hair, hazel eyes, fair complexion, brunette type, ht. 5-5, wt. 175, plump figure. Worth $3000. Desire companion of neat appearance.

291—I am a widow by death, positively of good character, do not smoke or drink, experienced in and enjoy home life, like to dress well, but not extravagant, enjoy the outdoors. English-American, high school education, age 52, medium brown hair, blue eyes, fair complexion, ht. 5-2, wt. 118. Own two properties. Good sense and morals, count most with me.

292—Have had years of experience as a housekeeper and cook, also in nursing. I have been told that I was fairly good looking and neat in appearance. American, Baptist, grade school education, age 40, brown hair, blue eyes, fair complexion, brunette, ht. 5-5, wt. 175. Own house and lot. Would like to hear from a gentleman 40 to 45, tall, dark hair and eyes.

293—American, protestant, grammar school education, age 48, black greying hair, brown eyes, medium fair complexion, ht. 5-3, wt. 135, neat figure. Am a widow, own my home, a nice, modern nine room home. I have a good, agreeable disposition, considered neat appearing, a good housekeeper and cook. Would not object to a poor man if he had a steady position.

294—I am a widow by death, good natured and easy to get along with, an excellent cook and good housekeeper. Irish descent, common school education, occupation farming, age 49, black greying hair, grey eyes, olive complexion, ht. 5-6, wt. 120, neat figure. Own 40 acre farm. Would like to hear from someone near my own height, good natured.

295—My friends tell me I do not show my age, that I look many years younger than I really am. I am a widow by death, have a good disposition, not bad looking, neat in dress and appearance. American, protestant, grade school education, age 50, chestnut brown hair, blue eyes, fair complexion, ht. 5-5, wt. 162. Own property worth $6000, will inherit.

296—I do not care for riches, just a congenial companion, home and happiness. Am very affectionate, believe in honesty, tolerant to other people's opinions, religion, etc. American, fair education, age 60, reddish brown greying hair, blue eyes, fair complexion, ht. 5-3, wt. 119, good figure. I own my home. Prefer a companion with high ideals, older than myself.

297—I am a home loving person, have a kind and affectionate disposition, like a good time in a nice way, like shows, do not smoke or drink, considered nice looking, like good clothes. American, protestant, common school education, age 56, blonde hair, blue eyes, fair complexion, ht. 5 ft., wt. 157. Worth about $5000. Wish to hear from a man of good habits.

298—Am a widow, very lonely for true companionship. I have a pleasant disposition, considered nice looking, am healthy, have a good, moral character. American, Baptist, grade school education, age 48, brown hair, blue eyes, fair complexion, ht. 5-2, wt. 140. I own a farm and need a good man to help me farm. Am good natured and easy to get along with.

299—All persons with whom I have come in contact have always admired my personal appearance, and good taste in choosing clothes and dressing. Irish descent, Catholic, good education, age 19, dark brown hair and eyes, fair complexion, ht. 5-5, wt. 118, very nice figure. Would like to correspond with young men of neat, dignified appearance, age 19 to 25. See my photo above.

300—I am a widow by death, considered nice looking, dress neatly and appropriately. Irish and French descent, protestant, well educated, age 47, mixed grey hair, brown eyes, medium fair complexion, ht. 5-6, wt. 148. Own a home and car. Wish to hear from a gentleman that is congenial, careful in dress.

301—I am considered good looking, very neat and attractive, dress very well. Am very broad-minded and sensible. I am an experienced typist, and have had some bookkeeping experience. Bohemian, Catholic, age 34, brown hair, hazel eyes, fair complexion, brunette, ht. 5-5, wt. 142. Have some means. Due to business experience, would like to hear from business man.

302—Not the best looking as far as physical features go, but considered attractive, neat and well dressed. Besides being a good cook and housekeeper, I am also an excellent seamstress. American, protestant, college education, school teacher, age 32, reddish brown hair, grey eyes, fair complexion, blonde type, ht. 5-7, wt. 138. Own some property.

303—Am a widow by divorce, considered good looking, have a pleasant disposition, a true friend and good pal. I have lived on a farm and in town, but prefer the country. American, protestant, high school education, age 36, black hair, blue eyes, light complexion, semi-brunette type, ht. 5-6, wt. 190. Worth $2000. Will consider matrimony with the right one.

304—I own a grocery store and meat market. I work in the store all day, get very lonely in the evening when work is done. Would prefer working at home, cooking and housekeeping. American, protestant, good education, age 65, brown greying hair, blue eyes, fair complexion, ht. 5-8, wt. 138. Worth $10,000. Want honest companion that can help in store.

305—Widow by death, all alone, no children. Have a friendly disposition, a good mixer with the right class of people. American, Baptist, common school education, age 55, brown grey-ing hair, hazel eyes, fair complexion, ht. 5-5½, wt. 150. Own a house and 40 acre farm. Would like to correspond with a Christian gentleman, one around 60 years of age.

306—I am not lazy, work every day and make my own living. I own my home, which is a 60 acre farm. I am a widow, considered nice looking, easy to get along with, very good disposition. American, protestant, fair education, age 45, light brown hair, blue-grey eyes, fair complexion, ht. 5-6, wt. 138. Wish to hear from a nice, true gentleman, one I can depend upon.

307—I am a widow by death, no children, do not drink or smoke, like all clean sports, especially swimming and fishing. Am neat and attractive, do not look my age. English and Irish, protestant, high school education, age 50, light brown hair, fair complexion, ht. 5-2, wt. 128. Own my home. The one of my choice must be fairly good looking and healthy.

308—People I meet are always friendly, and most of them tell me I have a nice disposition, and that I look young for my age. German-American, Lutheran, common school education, occupation farming, age 50, brown hair, blue eyes, fair complexion, ht. 5-2, wt. 122. Own a farm of 149 acres. I want a pal and life companion.

309—I like home and all it means. I enjoy outside interests, fishing, traveling, etc. Am of a happy disposition, have a neat appearance, like good clothes. English, Baptist, high school and one year college education, age 59, brown hair, grey eyes, olive complexion, ht. 5-5, wt. 150. Own my home and have comfortable living. Desire a companion near my age.

310—Kind, good natured, cheerful disposition, like clean fun, but do not smoke, drink or dance. Was born and raised on a farm, like country life. American, protestant, common school education, age 45, brown and gray hair, blue eyes, medium fair complexion, ht. 4-10, wt. 94. I own my home and furniture, four lots with fruit trees.

Chickenhouse Chronicles | 115

311—Considered excellent cook and housekeeper, neat and attractive, a Christian, do not smoke or drink, but do not condemn those who do in reason. Am content to spend most of my time at home. American, protestant, high school education, age 46, light brown hair, blue eyes, fair complexion, ht. 5 ft., wt. 108. Own 97 acre farm. Prefer man who would live on farm.

312—Pleasing personality, cheerful, respectable, nice looking, neat appearance, good dresser, have some talent in art and music. American, Catholic, two years academy, high school and business education, age 36, dark hair, brown eyes, medium fair complexion, brunette type, ht. 5-11, wt. 124. Some means. Desire companion of Catholic faith.

313—There is nothing unusual about myself, except that I am a hard worker. I own 48 acres of property, house and garage, clear of debt, and intend to start a turkey ranch. American, Episcopalian, high school education, age 42, black hair, brown eyes, fair complexion, ht. 5-2, wt. 127, perfect figure. Want a companion not afraid of work.

314—Considered nice looking and of neat appearance, good conversationalist, fine disposition, young looking for age. American, common school education, age 41, blonde hair, blue eyes, fair complexion, blonde type, ht. 5-2, wt. 105, nice figure. Own tourist cabins. Would have no objection to a poor man if nice looking and neat appearing.

315—Girlish figure, good looking, dress in the best of style, striking appearance, work with Church and Civic Clubs, liked by all for my magnetic personality, make friends with all I meet. Scotch-Irish, Methodist, high school education, age 52, dark brown hair, dark blue eyes, smooth, olive complexion, ht. 5-2, wt. 110. Apartment owner, good income.

316—Am living alone and am very lonely. I have a kind and considerate disposition, very sincere in this venture. I have many compliments on my neat personal appearance. American, protestant, high school education, age 48, dark brown hair and eyes, medium fair complexion, ht. 5-3, wt. 150. Own my home and car, occupied in taking care of my home.

317—Am considered a lady, like good society, have traveled considerably, have a fair education, considered attractive, well dressed, healthy, love to keep house and cook, home loving. American, protestant, high school education, office worker, age 44, auburn hair, blue eyes, fair complexion, ht. 5-6½, wt. 140, perfect figure. Own property worth $5000.

321—I am considered good looking although I am a very small type. My personal appearance is very nice, and am considered one of the well dressed girls in my community. American, Methodist, high school and two years college education, age 21, black hair, hazel eyes, light complexion, brunette type, ht. 4-11½, wt. 92. Wish to hear from a tall, fair looking young man. See my photo above.

318—I am alone, children married. I do not smoke or drink, yet I can mix in most any party. I love to dance, enjoy the great out of doors, flowers, fishing, hunting, drive a car. German-American, Lutheran, good education, nice looking, age 53, auburn hair, brown eyes, fair complexion, ht. 5 ft., wt. 118. Own income property worth $10,000.

319—My friends say I am a good neighbor, have a good personality, always jolly and friendly, treat everybody nice. American, Methodist, common school education, age 63, blonde hair, blue eyes, fair complexion, ht. 4-11, wt. 150. Own suburban property, a 6 room house and two acres of ground. Wish to hear from a nice, intelligent Christian gentleman.

320—Am very active, take part in all Church and Civic work, can lead study classes, girl scouts, preside at clubs. Am considered very neat, not bad looking. American, Methodist, two years college education, age 62, grey hair, blue eyes, fair complexion, ht. 5-4, wt. 135. Have a home and living. Desire a Christian companion, near my age.

322—Considered fairly good looking, have a good disposition, pleasing personality, a fairly good sense of humor, love outdoor sports, theatres and nice clothes. American, Catholic, high school education, beauty operator, age 27, light brown hair, blue eyes, medium fair complexion, brunette type, ht. 5-2½, wt. 110. Worth about $8000, fair salary.

323—I am considered good looking, good natured, good cook and housekeeper, like nice friends, do not like to drink, but will take a drink to be sociable. Scotch-Irish, Christian, high school education, age 52, grey hair, blue eyes, fair complexion, ht. 5-5½, wt. 164. Own my home. Interested in gentleman with fair income, likes to dance, good natured.

324—Good personality, pleasant, kind and affectionate, neat appearing dress nicely, like any kind of clean amusements, love home, like to travel. American, grammar school education, Presbyterian, nurse, age 54, brown greying hair, blue eyes, fair complexion, ht. 5-5, wt. 160. Own home in town, land out of town. Desire refined, Christian companion.

325—Am honest, sincere, good reputation, have a pleasing personality, sweet disposition, good health, dress neatly, a very good cook and housekeeper, plan wisely. American, Methodist, common school education, age 48, brown hair, grey eyes, fair complexion, ht. 5 ft., wt. 120. Have means. Wish to hear from a sober, industrious, clean cut gentleman.

326—Am honest, upright, and with a good reputation in the community in which I live. Considered a nice looking lady, with a good personality and can make friends easily. English, Baptist, common school education, occupation farming, age 65, brown hair and eyes, olive complexion, ht. 5-2, wt. 153. Own farm, have some money. Want companion of good moral character.

327—I am of good character, nice appearance, dress neat, look nice in clothes, intelligent, good cook and housekeeper. American, Baptist, high school education, seamstress, age 48, brown hair, blue eyes, light complexion, ht. 5-7, wt. 140. Have some means. Hope to find someone like myself who is lonely for the companionship of someone sincere and upright.

328—I am a widow by death, have one son six years of age. Would like to keep my home. American, Lutheran, grade school education, housewife and farmer, age 37, dark brown hair, blue eyes, light complexion, ht. 5-5, wt. 125. Own dairy farm with equipment, a car and some bonds. Would like to correspond with a gentleman 38 to 47, quiet, honest and true.

329—Most people like me because I have a gay disposition. I am not hard to please, could live in a tent and make a home. I like outdoor sports such as hunting and fishing. French descent, Baptist, grade school education, age 39, black hair, brown eyes, fair complexion, ht. 5-6½, wt. 125. Have means. Would like to hear from a farmer, one that likes livestock farming.

330—Am a widow by death, considered good looking and neat appearing, and people that do not know my age guess me to be about 25 years old. American, Methodist, grade school education, farming, age 38, light brown hair, blue eyes, fair complexion, ht. 5-3, wt. 140. I own 82 acres of land and new, eight room house. Desire a companion of good habits.

331—Have a jolly disposition, well liked by friends, neat and attractive in appearance, young looking for age. American, Christian, common school education, age 38, black hair, blue eyes, medium fair complexion, ht. 5-6, wt. 137, brunette type. Own 160 acres of land. Wish to hear from a gentleman that is honest and true.

332—Very attractive, intelligent, possess personality, neat appearing, have good business ability, industrious, have domestic inclinations. Holland Dutch, high school education, commercial artist, age 50, dark brown hair, brown eyes, olive complexion, ht. 5-6½, wt. 143, graceful shapely figure. In comfortable circumstances.

333—I try to be fair and honest in all dealings. I am a very good cook, like to have everything neat and tidy. American, grade school education, age 47, greying hair, brown eyes, fair complexion, ht. 5-5, wt. 145. Have home and income. Would like to correspond with a good, honest, Christian gentleman around 45 years of age.

335—Widow by death, very affectionate and tender hearted, of neat appearance, cheerful and pleasant, plenty of experience in cooking and keeping house. American, protestant, grade school education, age 44, brown hair, blue eyes, fair complexion, ht. 5-4, wt. 175. I own my home. Wish to hear from a pleasant, congenial gentleman.

334—Although I am rather stout, I try to dress stylishly and am very particular about my personal appearance. American, Presbyterian, two years high school education, beauty operator, own my shop. Age 33, reddish brown hair, dark brown eyes, fair complexion, brunette, ht. 5-3, wt. 152. Wish to hear from an honest, sober, refined gentleman 33 to 55. See my photo above.

336—Have owned and operated a jewelry store for the past 32 years. Considered neat and nice looking, wear clothes well, have a good personality, enjoy fishing, boating and swimming. American, Episcopalian, high school education, age 50, light brown hair, blue eyes, fair complexion, ht. 5-4, wt. 170. Own some property.

337—I am the home loving type, good disposition, very affectionate, always dressed in good taste, well experienced in all household duties. American, Lutheran, grammar school education, age 45, brown hair, hazel eyes, fair complexion, brunette, ht. 5-4, wt. 130, good figure, nice looking. Own property worth $3,000. The one of my choice need not be rich.

338—Widow, no children, very active, dance, swim, play violin, accomplished in a number of things, young looking for age. English, protestant, fair education, age 59, brown hair no grey, blue eyes, very fair complexion, ht. 5-4, wt. 130, good figure. Own home and car and other property worth $20,000. Matrimony in view if suited.

339—Neat personal appearance, well dressed, good personality, try to be a friend at all times, like the common things of life, not conceited. American, Baptist, grade school education, manager of cafe, age 41, brown hair, grey eyes, medium fair complexion, ht. 5-9, wt. 170. Own home in town and country. Desire someone near my height.

340—Considerate, have a jolly disposition, do not dance, smoke or drink. Am a widow by death, like clean living, love outdoor work. American, protestant, common school education, age 45, dark brown greying hair, brown eyes, clear, fair complexion, ht. 5-4½, wt. 170. Own home and other property. Farmer or stockman preferred.

341—I am a widow by death, considered nice looking for my age, a good dresser, like nice clothes. American, Baptist, common school education, age 57, blonde and grey hair, fair complexion, grey eyes, ht. 5-2½, wt. 175. Have some means. Would like to correspond with a congenial gentleman, one of the same religious faith if possible.

342—Amateur writer and poet, quiet, kind disposition, very ambitious and believe in work. Considered good looking, a neat dressed, fond of the great out-doors. German and English descent, Baptist, high school graduate, age 18, dark brown hair, blue-grey eyes, very fair complexion, ht. 5-6½, wt. 118. Will inherit a farm.

343—I have lived life fully and know what it is all about. Can enjoy and adapt myself to most ways of living. Considered stylish and attractive in appearance. American, college education, teacher, age 40, blonde hair, brown eyes, fair complexion, ht. 5-5½, wt. 125. Make good salary, buying home and car. Have talent in music.

344—American, common school education, fair looking, kind disposition, neat personal appearance, age 52, greying hair, blue eyes, fair complexion, ht. 5-8, wt. 160. Own my home. Would like to correspond with a gentleman of affectionate disposition, one who likes to go places and have good times, such as dances and shows.

Lady members are required to answer or return all letters containing stamp, this is a strict rule of this club and must be complied with.

WOULD YOU MARRY?

If you want us to take charge of your case, give it personal attention and assist you in finding a suitable companion, send us a complete description of yourself, the kind of wife you want, and five dollars, and we will agree to send you descriptions, names and addresses until you are married.

You will receive copies of all catalogues, lists etc., each and every month, upon receipt of your membership certificate, together with postage. Your ad will be published in the next issue, therefore, a $5.00 membership is just what you want and is the best and cheapest in the end. Please return the enclosed order blank with either $2.00 for a twelve months' membership, or $5.00 for a membership good until suited.

NOTHING SUCCEEDS LIKE SUCCESS.

THE FACT THAT OUR BUSINESS IS A SUCCESSFUL ONE is a guarantee to you that it is carried on honestly. We could not exist long otherwise. Truth and Fair and Square Dealing is Our Aim.

IF YOU ARE IN EARNEST, WE WILL ASSIST YOU.

No matter what your position in life may be, there will be a tide in your affairs which, if taken at its flood, leads on to fortune. If you are a man of intelligence and business capacity, but lack capital to start in business, you could, by marrying a woman with money, start yourself on the road to independence. But do not lose sight of the fact that it does not always take money to make a person happy. We have lady advertisers that may not have a dollar to their name, but are worth their weight in gold as a life companion.

NO ADDRESSES WILL BE FURNISHED FREE.

It is utterly useless and only a waste of your time and ours to ask for free names and addresses, or request us to forward your letters to parties whose descriptions are printed in this book. This we wish to be distinctly understood. The only way you can get names and addresses is to send the amount mentioned elsewhere in this book.

ADVERTISEMENTS ARE GENUINE.

Every personal advertisement appearing in these columns is genuine, the application blank filled out and signed by the lady advertising, is on file in this office and is held as a proof of insertion and as a voucher for the genuineness of every advertisement of a lady published by THE EXCHANGE.

We also wish to state, that each lady whose advertisement you see here, has signed a statement in which she agrees to answer or return all letters received from gentlemen when postage is enclosed.

We publish all ads as we receive them and orders for memberships are filled by return mail.

By sending in your certificate with postage each month, you can obtain a list of lady advertisers that have just joined the club, in fact we print their ads as fast as we receive new applications for membership.

SPECIAL NOTICE

We desire it fully understood by every reader of this booklet that all statements of personal advertisers are the statements of the advertisers, without regard to the wording. The publisher of this booklet has made no investigation into the truth or falsity of the advertisers' statements as to their financial or other standing, education, character, profession or occupaion, and under no circumstances will the publisher guarantee the accuracy of any statement, or assume any responsibility therefor, by reason of the appearance of such statements in this booklet. We simply act as agents.

IF YOU WANT TO MEET NEW FRIENDS TAKE THIS CHANCE TO GET ACQUAINTED NOW!

Why be lonely, friends? Why miss out on the good times you could be sharing with others who have the same tastes, same love of fun and companionship? When all the time there is such a simple way to meet other lonely people who are as anxious as you to get to know new friends and acquaintances—even buddies or sweethearts?

You just have to sit down and write a letter to someone else. That's all. Someone who may need cheering up, or a friend to talk things over with. Many, many people have made enduring friendships that started just this way. You can, too.

You say you are too shy, don't know how to go about it, are not so sure it's "the right thing to do." As far as being shy is concerned, meeting people through friendly letters is much easier than meeting them in person —you learn to know them slowly and easily, and take your time getting used to them between letters. And it's such fun to get letters!

As time goes on, your friendship may ripen and hold great things in store for you. You and your friends may want to meet, and find mutual personal interests that make you permanent pals. Each of you may have other friends you want to introduce to each other. See how easy it is? No need to feel shy! And the postman's visits can become a real treat.

Letter-writing is simple, too. You simply get our lists of descriptions, names and addresses each month of people to write to. Then you choose any names with descriptions that appeal to you or sound like they would be fun to know. The people in these ads want you to write—that's why they are trying to reach you through The Exchange.

Who knows what the future will hold for you then? Romance? Love? Perhaps everything you have longed for to make your life full and happy— and all because you have given yourself the chance to get acquainted with other lonely men or women this easy exciting way!

Think of it! In a short while you may be writing to the person who can make you the happiest man or woman on earth! No more loneliness! But someone who will love and cherish you, and make your dreams come true.

What's more important, you gain a new interest in life—meet people outside your own community who may have many unusual experiences or hobbies or activities to tell you about and share with you. And you see, you have much to give others, too, no matter how unimportant your own doings seem to you.

Think of how you will enjoy getting those letters. The first ones will feel like a warm handshake. It will do your heart good to know you have "met" others in places you might never get to in person. Of course, you can exchange snapshots, too, so you can enjoy seeing your new friends in pictures.

After reading this, we are sure you will ask yourself, "Why be lonely," and sit right down and do something about it! And your future will surely hold new interest for you—which you may never have found otherwise.

Foremost Matrimonial Magazine in the World

Cupid's Columns

Established 1891.

Volume 59, Number 1   JANUARY-FEBRUARY, 1950   Price 10 Cents

LADIES

604 Wash.—Widow, 45, 5 ft. 9 in., 160 lbs., light brown hair, blue eyes. Am good cook, keep clean house, good hearted, nice looking. I love sports and shows. Don't drink or smoke, will live anywhere. Wish to correspond with man who will make a good husband and who will care for a home and my boy.

474 Minn.—Single girl, Methodist, 45, 5 ft. 2 in., 115 lbs., brown hair and eyes. Doesn't smoke or drink. Am a bookkeeper, have 1 year college. Wishes to correspond with kind refined man near own age.

Dec. 16, 1949

Dear Editor:
I take pleasure in announcing the marriage of —— to ——. Yes, Sir, thanks to your "Cupid's Columns" we found each other, and we were married in November and we are happy as can be. You may discontinue sending the publication to the two above mentioned addresses.
We are both thankful that we found Cupid's Columns.
Sincerely,
C. G.

LADIES

608)a.—I am a divorcee in my fifties, 5 ft. 3 in., have brown eyes and hair. I am a good cook and housekeeper. I am looking for a gentleman over 50 who has some capital he would consider investing in a small jewelry store. No objection if physically handicapped.

607 Virginia—I am widow, 57, 4 ft. 11 in., 160 lbs., with brown hair, blue eyes. English descent, high school education, housewife, and own my own home. I like to write letters, church activities, and would try to please man I married. Would like to correspond with sober, honest, sincere man who is financially able to support a wife.

603 Wash. D. C.—Divorcee, 49, 5 ft. 8 in., slender, wishes to correspond with gentleman 50-65, well-bred. I am teacher with college education, A.B. and M.D. Degrees, Episcopal. Live in Wash. D. C., and like art, theater, novel, collecting, cooking and conversational books. Kindly send picture which will be returned.

461 Tenn.—Widow, 58, 5 ft. 1 in., 170 lbs., brunette, brown eyes. Own home, new Oldsmobile, nice income, no debts. Want to meet a man near my own age, 6 ft., similar circumstances, clean, honest, intelligent, nice looking, Protestant, doesn't drink or smoke, active, dependable, affectionate, kind, good dresser. Stamp and photo with letter.

LADIES

605 Virginia—I am divorced, 54, 5 ft. 4 in., 200 lbs., with gray hair and brown eyes. Protestant, with high school education. Employed as a hotel room clerk, $35 a week. Own my home, don't drink or smoke. Am good tempered but have serious disposition, like baseball and football, and especially bridge. Wish to correspond with man, 55-65, 175-200 lbs., 5 ft. 5 in.-6 ft., who is nondrinker and likes church activities and sports.

606 Ohio—American Baptist widow, 63, 5 ft. 7 in., 200 lbs., fair complexion, gray hair, and blue eyes. Active and attractive seamstress. Don't drink or smoke. Good cook and nice house-keeper, sunny disposition, dresses well, loves home. Wishes to correspond with congenial, sincere, home-loving man, neat dresser, any age, city, or country.

610 Minneapolis—Single lady, 39, 5 ft. 7 in., 134 lbs., brown hair, hazel eyes. Danish descent, Lutheran. High school education, steadily employed. Quiet nature, enjoys home life, neat and conservative. Do not smoke or drink. Likes music, movies, reading. Wishes to correspond with Protestant man, 40-50, 5 ft. 8 in. to 6 ft., who enjoys home life, does not drink. Is respectable, clean, honest, sincere. Someone living in or near Mpls., Minn., or cities in Calif. Not interested in farmer.

LADIES

609 Wisc.—Widow, 48, 5 ft. 3 in., 160 lbs., brown hair, blue eyes, nice appearance, and disposition. Have daughter 13. Lutheran, good habits, honest and reliable. Wishes kind hearted, reliable, honest man, 48-60, who would give a good home and security to worthy woman. Must have high ideals. No gambler or drunkard. Please send photo in first letter.

471 Minneapolis—I am neat dresser, good cook. Pleasant, very lonely, want to marry. Like home life, fishing, dancing, swimming, music. Widow, 56, 5 ft. 5 in., 160 lbs., gray hair, brown eyes, fair complexion. Wishes to correspond with man clean, honest, near own age or younger, no drinker, who has steady job or other means that can help on small resort. Owns summer resort.

Dec. 14, 1949

Dear Editor:
Please discontinue sending Cupid's Columns to me. It has served its purpose and is a wonderful magazine.
Respectfully,
O. P.

CUPID'S COLUMNS

LADIES

author's mother

472 N.Y.—Charming, attractive, pretty, refined brunette, 28, 5 ft. 4½ in., 129 lbs. College educated. Plays piano and sings. I am wonderful cook and h o u s e k e e p e r. Know how to farm or ranch. Would love to correspond with farmer or rancher, or any respectable gentleman who loves children. I have 4 children, 7, 5, 3, 1. Would like to meet someone who would sincerely love my children and make them his own and be a good father to them, since they lost their own. My children would be a great help to a farmer or rancher in later years, however any gentleman who thinks he could love my children will be considered. Am willing to go anyplace in the world for the right man.

351 Virginia — Nice-looking widow, 55, 5 ft. 2½ in., 112 lbs., brown hair and eyes. Kind, even-tempered, likes clean fun and church work. Wishes to meet sober, refined, jolly Christian man who has home. She will do everything to make a worthy man happy.

353 South Dakota—I am a widow, 59, 5 ft. 2 in., 123 lbs. I have no bad habits, have a sunny disposition, good health. I am English-German descent, a Methodist, gray eyes, dark graying hair. Former school teacher, now a clerk; I own my home. Wish to meet man of similar background.

372 Rochester, N. Y.—Refined widow, 45, 5 ft. 2 in., 106 lbs., black hair, grey eyes, fair looks. Wants to hear from refined gentleman of good family. I am a real good sport, looking for a real pal. I am from a good family; Protestant. Have some cash. I am alone, please write.

370 Minneapolis.—Widow, 50, 5 ft. 2 in., 132 lbs., dark brown hair, blue eyes. Protestant; French-English descent. Machine operator. Doesn't drink. Attractive, good dresser; likes all outdoor sports. Affectionate. Wishes to meet man near own age, loyal true sincere

affectionate
140 lbs., red
Owns floral
me. Smokes,
ekeeper and
g. Wishes to
e-loving man
55, no drink-

ıg widow, 58,
brown hair,
actical nurse
ood income.
rds, doesn't
car. Wishes
ge, of good
around 165
ort wife and

ears old, but
and am very
I am look-
ho would be
e, dress well,
ve an income
eran.

ft. 8 in., gray
drink, smoke.
ousekeeping.
lly man who

. Y.—I would
ing wife and
sekeeper for
d man. I am
8, 5 ft. 3 in.,
Irish-Catho-
like dancing,
ovies, but
king most of
ld like to cor-
with jolly,
atholic man,
ion to a wid-

9, 4 ft. 11 in.,
s. Good cook,
s music, all
Minnesota.
es to corres-
astes.

n Kentucky

373
5 ft. 2 i
Luthera
trailer.
to corre
55, goo

368
widow,
and eye
tical nu
tured, :
She is
man pr

466
106 lbs.,
plexion,
drink, h
likes da
like to
ests.

436
5 ft., 1
descent,
to find :
fer a fa
or not r
ways.
a good

433
in., 190
month
good ho
would li
home li
woman

392
lady, 42
blue eye
cook ar
respond
with go

435
blue eye
5 ft. 1
English

has pro
home
d a n c i
meet se
gentle
neat, a

Due to format complications it was not practical to print all the lonely hearts publications that the author discovered in the old farmhouse attic. Below is the full list of singles publications.

1945-12-13 The Exchange

1946-03-13 Exchange Publishing

1946-06-01 Exchange Publishing

1946-08-01 Standard Correspondence Club

1947-02-20 Certificate of Service

1950-01-01Standard Correspondence Club

1950-01-03 Cupid's Columns

For the reader interested in exploring the historical catalogues, including hundreds of the women's names, go to http://www.wendellaffield.com/books PDF download $2.99

Also included, a preview chapter of:

The Farm 1950s
Chickenhouse Chronicles: Book II,
http://www.whisperingpetalspress.com/books

WENDELL AFFIELD

Wendell Affield, the third of nine children born to Barbara Affield, grew up on a small farm in northern Minnesota. He was born in NYC and moved to Minnesota, as a toddler in 1949, when his mother met his stepfather, Herman Affield, through *Cupid's Columns*. In 1960 Affield, twelve at the time, and his siblings were placed in foster homes after his mother was committed to Fergus Falls State Hospital. At sixteen Affield left home, rode the rails and lived in hobo camps.

At seventeen Affield enlisted in the navy. He was mid-way through his first tour in Vietnam in 1966 when he was emancipated by Beltrami County Juvenile Court; it was also the year his class graduated from high school. In January 1968 Affield returned to Vietnam as the cox'n of a river patrol boat with the Mobile Riverine Force. On August 18, 1968 he was wounded in an ambush and medevaced home.

After leaving the navy in 1969, he found work as a meat cutter apprentice in the Chicago area. A few years later he became a manager, a position he held with various companies for almost thirty years. In 1980 he and his family returned to northern Minnesota. After retiring in 2001 Affield enrolled in Bemidji State University, where, over the years, his Vietnam essays evolved into *Muddy Jungle Rivers* (2012).

In 2010 after his mother died, Affield discovered a treasure trove of family history locked in the chickenhouse of the farm he was raised on—letters dating back to 1822. He also discovered a series of 1940s singles publications that his stepfather ordered after returning from

WWII. *Herman, 1940s Lonely Hearts Search, Chickenhouse Chronicles Book*, published in 2017, is based on those discoveries.

Today, remembering his homeless time while riding the rails and living in hobo camps as a youth, Affield volunteers at Bemidji Community Food Shelf. He works on his *Chickenhouse Chronicles* series, speaks to veteran groups about PTSD, and leads a Veteran's Writer Group at his local VA Clinic. He is a 2017 recipient of Minnesota Humanities Center "Veteran's Voices Award" for his work with the underserved in his community. He and his wife, Patti, live in northern Minnesota. They have two children and several grandchildren. Sadly, their son, Jeffry, died in 2015.

ALSO BY WENDELL AFFIELD

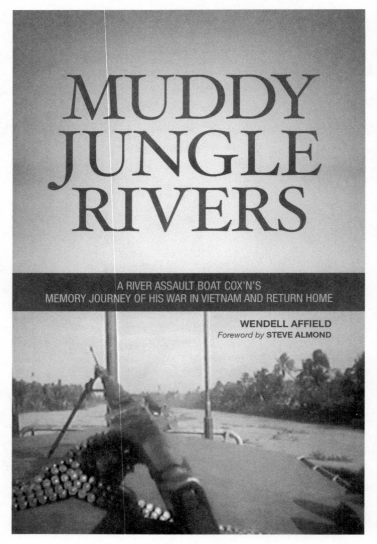

MUDDY JUNGLE RIVERS

A RIVER ASSAULT BOAT COX'N'S
MEMORY JOURNEY OF HIS WAR IN VIETNAM AND RETURN HOME

WENDELL AFFIELD
Foreword by **STEVE ALMOND**

Order at:
Wendellaffield.com/books